The Cashmere Shawl

Monique Lévi-Strauss

The Cashmere Shawl

Photographs by
Massimo Listri

DRYAD PRESS LIMITED   LONDON

Opposite title page: *The Persian*.
France, 1815–30.
Painted papier mâché, height
205 cm/6 ft 9 in.
Paris, Musée Carnavalet, no.
EN 51.

This statue was the sign of a
shop on the corner of the rue
de Richelieu and the rue de
la Bourse in Paris which sold
cashmere shawls and lace.
In one of the novels of the
Comédie Humaine, Balzac
describes the "*comédie des
cachemires*" which was played
out in this famous shop.

In the dimensions of shawls given on pages 53–181 the
first measurement is always that of the warp length,
excluding the fringe. Unless otherwise indicated, the
shawls are woven in one piece.

Copyright © 1986 Arnoldo Mondadori Editore
S.p.A., Milan
Mondadori International
English translation copyright © 1987
Arnoldo Mondadori Editore S.p.A., Milan
Translated by Sara Harris

ISBN 0852I 9759 4
First published in Great Britain in 1987
by Dryad Press Limited
   8 Cavendish Square
   London WIM OAJ

Photoset by Rowland Phototypesetting Limited
Bury St Edmunds, Suffolk
Printed and bound in Italy by Arnoldo Mondadori
Editore S.p.A., Verona for the publishers, Dryad
Press Limited

Contents

Preface

In the early 1950s my husband and I used to go to the Paris Flea Market, lured by our love of the unusual. In those days our purchases were of necessity mainly utilitarian. But what a marvellous time that was, when we could eat our meals off a dinner service made at Creil-Montereau a century earlier but which cost no more than new china; when I used to wrap a cashmere shawl (which had once been the pride and joy of some nineteenth-century aristocratic lady) around myself like a cloak in the evenings. I was able to buy these shawls very cheaply as it was not worth the dealers' while to restore them. Often all it took was a wash in cold water to bring the glowing colours back to life and restore the much sought after caressing warmth of the soft goat's fleece. Sometimes I had to try my hand at being a textile restorer, a difficult but very rewarding job. Repairing these shawls and wearing them led me to wonder when and where they had been woven. Enquiries of the dealers and even of textile experts proved fruitless, so I decided to turn to written sources for the answers, knowing how much the women of the previous century had coveted them and what an enormous expense such a purchase was for the men who had to pay for them: in those days a cashmere shawl would have cost the same price as a mink coat today.

It did not take me long to consult all the relevant catalogue entries and read all the books listed under the headings *Cashmere* and *Shawls* at the Bibliothèque Nationale, the Bibliothèque Forney, the Musée des Arts Décoratifs and the Musée Guimet. While such travellers as François Bernier (1664), Victor Jacquemont (1831) and Carl von Hügel (1836) were not experts on the subject, they have provided us with valuable descriptions of the technique of cashmere shawl weaving. From Jean Rey (1823), a historian and shawl manufacturer, we learn how the Paris shawl industry operated and the European techniques employed to copy Oriental shawls. Another shawl manufacturer, E. F. Hébert, depicted the life of a Parisian shawl weaver in an 1857 monograph entitled "Tisseur en châles à Paris" published by F. Le Play which Mme Claudine Reinharez (an expert on costume) very kindly suggested I should read soon after I first embarked on my quest.

No layman could, however, hope to understand the terminology used in these descriptions of the techniques and tools of the craft, especially in the absence of any illustrations. They would only be intelligible to someone already well versed in the subject. In short, more questions were raised than answered. Three albums of shawl designs were extant, devoid of any explanatory text, compiled by Fleury Chavant (1837 and 1839) and by Victor Delaye (prior to 1867). In addition both the Cabinet des Dessins of the Musée des Arts Décoratifs and the Musée des Techniques of the Conservatoire National des Arts et Métiers housed good collections of drawings of shawls.

No links were, however, apparent between these texts without pictures, the pictures without text and the unattributed shawls which we were studying. It was perhaps this gap which in 1955 prompted John Irwin (at that time keeper of the Indian Section at London's Victoria and Albert Museum), to write a book entitled *Shawls, A Study in Indo-European Influences.* The author traces the history of Kashmir shawls and nineteenth-century European copies of them. Thirty-six plates showed examples of the Oriental weavers' production, while 15 were of shawls manufactured in Britain: in Norwich, Edinburgh and Paisley. One of these British examples, plate no. 50, shows a long shawl with a white background from a private collection which is attributed to Paisley manufacture, and dates from about 1850. It is, however, identical to the pattern by the French designer A. Berrus, shown on page 99 of this book, except for the horizontal border and the harlequin fringe. So was this shawl woven in Paisley after all? This is just one of many unsolved mysteries which may well continue to elude researchers, so jealously did the manufacturers guard their trade secrets. In publishing over 50 illustrations of shawls, each with explanatory text giving a date and place of origin, John Irwin was bravely laying himself open to correction and thus earned the reputation of pioneering spirit among students of the history of Kashmir shawls in Europe. Even if some of its dates have subsequently had to be revised, John Irwin's book opened up a new area of research, into the cross-fertilization of influences between the Far East and Europe during the nineteenth century, of which shawls provide one of the best examples. In 1973, his first book long out of print, Irwin produced a second, revised edition, published under the title *The Kashmir Shawl*. Eight additional plates were included, showing boteh patterns brought back from India by Moorcroft in 1823, now in the Metropolitan Museum, New York; eight new illustrations of cashmere shawls were also included but all the examples of shawls from Norwich, Edinburgh and Paisley were omitted.

Although I was familiar with the relevant books and documents, I was still at a loss to date or find a provenance for the shawls I found at antique dealers' shops, auction rooms or in private hands; I was, moreover, unable to equate the nineteenth-century terminology with the various types of shawls. I decided, therefore, to approach the Musée Historique des Tissus in Lyons, which I regarded as the Mecca of the textile world. I duly wrote to the Museum and it was agreed that I should meet the keeper, Jean-Michel Tuchsherer and his technical assistant, Gabriel Vial, who had taught at the Ecole de Tissage, Lyons. The former soon dashed my hope by bursting out laughing: "Kashmir shawls? We know absolutely nothing about them. In fact, if you want to write something on the subject, I'll gladly publish it." He very kindly allowed me to examine the shawls stored in the museum together with M. Vial and another assistant curator, Mlle Odile Valansot. Gabriel Vial did his best to explain the technical differences between shawls from the two continents. In return I was able to give him some information which I had gleaned in the course of my reading on the subject. We agreed to meet again.

The opportunity presented itself a few months later, through Mme Krishna Riboud, an expert on ancient Chinese textiles, who had been collecting Asian materials for 30 years. She had just founded the A.E.D.T.A., *Association pour l'Etude et la Documentation des Textiles d'Asie*, and she invited M. Vial and me to go and examine her collection of shawls, most of which come from Kashmir and nearby regions. M. Vial's comments shed new light on some obscure sections of the historical texts which I had failed to understand when reading them. We subsequently spent days at a time studying shawls together, in the company of Mlle Valansot. I should like to pay tribute to M. Vial's knowledge and to express my appreciation of his generosity in sharing it with me. Had Mme Riboud and he not given me so much encouragement, I would probably have abandoned the project.

M. Vial introduced me to Mme Christiane Lassalle, keeper of the Musée du Vieux Nîmes. This museum occupies the former bishop's palace and houses in its collections about 100 cashmere shawls. These are aired once a year, during the month of May; it was therefore suggested that this would be a suitable time for Mlle Valansot, M. Vial and myself to inspect them. The majority were of European origin; Nîmes ranked third among the centers of the French shawl industry and a number of the examples we were shown were produced there, so I was able to have a good idea of a typical Nîmes shawl.

Once I had collated all the facts from the books I had read and the information which the shawls themselves had given me, I decided to explore the textile collections of the Paris museums. I found shawls in the Asian Department of the Musée de l'Homme; in the Costume Department of the Musée des Arts et Traditions Populaires; in the Textile Department of the Musée des Arts Décoratifs and, more predictably, at the Musée de la Mode et du Costume de la Ville de Paris where Mlle Madeleine Delpierre was then head keeper. She spent nearly two hours showing me about 30 shawls which she had assembled from the museum's reserves, held in storage in various parts of the city. It was then that I had the idea of exhibiting the museum's shawls. I planned to complete the display by asking the A.E.D.T.A. to loan some Kashmir shawls, and by drawing on other collections. After several weeks' consideration, Mlle Delpierre agreed to mount an exhibition of shawls in the spring of 1982.

Louis Lomüller, the historian, had just published an impressive biography of the industrialist Guillaume Ternaux who, during the first third of the nineteenth century, became famous as a shawl manufacturer. I wrote to M. Lomüller who gave me a list of Ternaux's descendants. Mlle Delpierre contacted them to ask whether they had any shawls woven by their ancestor. We were lent four shawls, which had been handed down through the family, for the forthcoming exhibition; two of these matched the description of shawls ordered from Ternaux in 1811 by Napoleon. It was our first success.

We knew of the existence, in the Victoria and Albert Museum, of a French shawl which had caused a sensation at the 1839 Exhibition. The museum was willing to lend it to us. W. E. Hefford, assistant keeper of the Textile Department, had identified the shawl from a reproduction of its original design drawing which appeared in a contemporary publication, *Souvenir de l'Exposition de 1839*. It had been woven by Gaussen to a design by A. Couder who had called it the *Nou-Rouz* (page 82). N. K. Rothstein, deputy keeper of the department, discovered the original design for the shawl hanging on the wall of a staircase in the Conservatoire National des Arts et Métiers in Paris. These two colleagues of John Irwin have studied the superb European shawls which the Victoria and Albert Museum acquired in the course of the last century. They managed to identify a number of them; one was attributable to Bournhonet, Ternaux's successor, and they authorized the reproduction here of the illustration on page 81. More pressing work has so far prevented them from publishing the fruits of their research, but when this does appear, it is sure to prove very enlightening.

The object of the exhibition at the Musée de la Mode et du Costume was to postulate a chronology. The two Ternaux shawls, together with the Gaussen shawl lent by the Victoria and Albert Museum, were vital proof but they were not enough. A number of signed and dated shawl designs were borrowed from the Conservatoire National des Arts et Métiers and the Musée des Arts Décoratifs. Fashion plates and portraits, all dated and which could be tied in with extant shawls, meant that there was supporting evidence for our demonstration.

The Musée de l'Impression sur Etoffes in Mulhouse possesses both woven and printed cashmere shawls. This Museum also houses a wealth of accessible archive material which facilitates the identification of locally printed shawls. The identification of European shawls from other soúrces (Normandy, Provence, Britain) is more problematical. Under the supervision of Mme Jacqueline Jacqué, the keeper, a second exhibition of shawls took place in Mulhouse in February 1983. In December of that same year a third exhibition opened at the Musée Historique des Tissus in Lyons under the aegis of the present keeper, M. Pierre Arizzoli-Clémentel. Gerolamo Etro of Milan lent his *Nou-Rouz* shawl to both these later exhibitions.

My aim in all three exhibitions was the same: to show the host museum's entire collection of cashmere shawls and to demonstrate to the visiting public how the designs and the various techniques had evolved. No catalogue was published for the Mulhouse exhibition but those for Paris and Lyons now constitute the inventories of the two museums' collections. My investigations over the years had enabled me to draw up a rough chronology (many entries being tentative) which nevertheless proved helpful to keepers wishing to date items in their textile collections. I relied on each exhibition to put my classification to the test and confirm my methodology by exposing mistakes. Errors were inevitable. As each exhibition came and went I aimed, ideally, to correct dates where necessary or at least to reduce margins of error. There were also some unexpected corroborations, such as occur when a shawl can be linked with a dress of known date, dispelling any remaining doubts.

During the last ten years or so, a number of books on cashmere shawls have been published. In Japan two major works have appeared, showing shawls in private collections. Ed Rossbach, who taught textile design in California, has analyzed the West's various interpretations of the cashmere style in his book entitled *The Art of Paisley*. By combining illustrations with informative text and commentary, all these publications add to our knowledge and make it possible to identify shawls which were previously unclassifiable.

When I was asked to write a book on the subject in January 1986 I accepted enthusiastically. This was the first opportunity I had had to publish a large number of colour plates. I was, however, loath to write a book which would add little to previous coverage of the subject. In order to avoid this, I decided to limit the historical and geographical scope of the book and, except where this was unavoidable, to exclude illustrations which had already appeared elsewhere. To forestall possible criticism on this score, I should like to underline that there are deliberate gaps in my treatment of the subject.

In the Indian subcontinent, and in Kashmir in particular, shawls have been woven for centuries. The great Indian collections, at the Victoria and Albert Museum, the Museum of Fine Arts in Boston and the A.E.D.T.A. in Paris, to mention only a few of the most outstanding, possess shawls or fragments of shawls woven in Kashmir before 1800. Kashmir's role in fashion and in the European textile industry is, however, limited to the nineteenth century. I shall, therefore, confine myself to this period of the history of the Kashmir shawl, and to French production. I made a considered decision to concentrate on shawl making in France although important shawl industries also flourished in other European countries, such as Britain (initially in Edinburgh and Norwich and later in Paisley); Austria (in Vienna) and Germany, where production centered on Elderfeld, and Russia.

I had good reason for limiting my coverage in this way: British, Austrian and German manufacturers were inspired by the French designers' products, just as the Lyons and Nîmes producers looked to Paris. This relationship did not change throughout the period in question. Limiting myself to a study of French shawl designs is not, therefore, so restrictive as it might first appear. It will then be up to specialists in each country, following on from contribution, to research documentary evidence for their own national shawl industries and publish the results. My coverage of such areas would have been limited to secondary sources; details of previous publications are listed in the bibliography at the end of this book. Since publishing considerations meant that only a set number of pages was available, I thought it preferable to reproduce the greatest possible number of previously unpublished, reliably authenticated French examples and documentation rather than cover more ground superficially.

Although I have isolated the history of French shawl production from that of other European countries, I could not separate it from that of Kashmir: their development was closely linked throughout the whole of the nineteenth century. In this book we move from France to Kashmir and back, as the story unfolds.

Unlike their British counterparts, French museums did not buy shawls at the time of the great national or international exhibitions. Those now in the French state collections were given or bequeathed to them, with no information as to their provenance. This reveals the low esteem in which nineteenth-century industrial arts were held for so long in France. Fortunately, signed and dated original shawl designs were conserved by two Paris museums. The Cabinet des Dessins of the Musée des Arts Décoratifs was given all the design drawings and gouaches from Berrus's studio by his widow; hundreds of pencil drawings, bound in albums can be studied there by arrangement. Dozens of other outline designs by Berrus and Gonelle are filed in drawers. The keeper of the Cabinet des Dessins, Marie-Noël de Gary was kind enough to let me have access to this collection whenever I wished. The other collection of designs belongs to the Conservatoire National des Arts et Métiers; they are hung on a staircase which is closed to the public. These designs, about 30 in all, are signed Couder, Berrus and Sevray. The earliest dates from 1823 and the latest from 1878; they were all exhibited at the national industrial exhibitions. It is vital to refer back to such evidence in order to understand how the style of shawls evolved.

It is all too apparent that the designs of other, less famous names are now lost to us, since the number and variety of extant shawls is greater than those recorded by surviving designs. What can be asserted with confidence is that those design drawings we are lucky enough to be able to publish in this book exerted significant influence on the development of style. I should like to thank Michèle Bachelet of the Conservatoire National des Arts et Métiers who allowed me access to the famous staircase over many years and authorized the publication of Amédée Couder's handwritten *Notices Explicatives*, concerning three of his designs which had at one time been exhibited and which she found in the museum's archives.

In studying the design drawings reproduced here, the reader may wonder why only one square shawl design has been included. The reason is that this example was the only design drawing of its type to be exhibited; it dates from 1834, when square shawls enjoyed greater popularity than long shawls because they were better suited to the cut of contemporary clothes. The Berrus albums contain dozens of pencil and pen and ink designs for square shawls, but long shawls were endowed with more prestige.

I gave up my original idea of draping most of shawls when they were photographed. I realized that although the smaller decorative motifs would still be visible, in spite of the folds, the larger motifs would be obscured by shadows and the overall impression of the design composition would be lost. I have to admit that when smoothed out flat a Kashmir shawl loses much of its allure.

To those who would like to know more about the origins and symbolism of the pine (*boteh*, as it is known in Kashmir) I can offer the following brief explanation: this motif probably first appeared in Persia or India but there is such controversy on the subject that it is very difficult to opt for any one of the many hypotheses. Much has been written about its probable significance, from "tree of life" to "mango," with others opting for "cypress" and "palm" on the way and it probably serves no purpose to choose one among so many. I have used the term pine throughout the book as this was the term most widely used in the English-speaking world and forms part of the currently accepted vocabulary. I have opted for the term pine throughout the book since it is most widely used in the English-speaking world, and I gratefully acknowledge Wendy Hefford's help in providing English equivalents for the specific terms related to the shawl industry.

My thanks go to Frédérique Delbecq, Director of the A.E.D.T.A., Annie Vallantin, assistant to Marie-Noël de Gary at the Musée des Arts Décoratifs, and Annaluisa Cameli who gave us access to the Etro collection in Milan; the help they all gave to Massimo Listri when he photographed the shawls, patterns and designs at their workplaces was invaluable.

I should also like to express my heartfelt gratitude to those mentioned in this introduction, who opened their doors and allowed me to study their collections; they gave me much encouragement on more than one occasion. Finally, I wish to thank all those (too numerous to list here) with whom I have corresponded, friends and strangers alike and from whom I have gained so much information. I could not have written this book without their help. It will all, I am sure, continue to prove must fruitful in completing my project. This book is merely an interim report, as it were, on work in progress.

Monique Lévi-Strauss

Opposite: "Indian shawl made by Chambellan & Duché, Paris, cashmere style border, detail of shawl pattern." Plate no. 17 from the album *Souvenir de l'Exposition des Produits de l'Industrie Française de 1839* (Souvenir album of the 1839 Exhibition of the Products of French industry). Paris, Bibliothèque Forney.

This drawing was for a square shawl with Muslim, Persian and Chinese-style motifs, the border retaining a typically cashmere design.

From India to Europe

Origins

Kashmir is bounded on the east by China, to the north by the Soviet Union, and on the west by Pakistan. The capital, Srinagar, lies in the Kashmir valley which is only just over 150 kilometers/93 miles long and 30 kilometers/18 miles wide. The foothills of the Himalayas rise high above Kashmir (which is situated at an average altitude of 1,800 meters/4,875 feet) forming an enclosed basin, watered by the River Jhelum and its numerous tributaries. The river forms a lake in the center of the plain and then flows on southwards until it reaches the Punjab valley.

In this fertile valley with its terraced rice fields grow fruit trees, poplars, plane trees, cypresses and cedars. Sheep and goats are reared beneath snow-capped peaks towering more than 8,000 m/26,000 ft high, which are mirrored in the calm, wide waters of the River Jhelum. Flowers abound, particularly roses and rhododendrons, whence comes the popular description of Kashmir as "the paradise of India." Kashmir had already been invaded many times when, in the mid fourteenth century, the Muslims succeeded in wresting the province from its Indian overlords. In 1586 it was conquered by Akbar, the great Moghul emperor. In 1739 the Kashmiris were forced to accept the Afghans as their masters, followed in 1819 by the Sikhs led by Ranjit Singh. In 1846 Gulab Singh, Rajah of Lahore, signed a treaty with the British by which they recognized his title to territories extending over mountainous areas of some 218,000 sq. km/76,600 sq. mi, including Kashmir. Gulab Singh was succeeded by Rambhir Singh, in whose reign the 1846 charter defining the respective rights of the British and Kashmiris was renewed. Rambhir Singh was to pay an annual tribute to Queen Victoria consisting of a horse, 25 pounds of wool and three pairs of shawls. In return Britain acknowledged the Rajah's right to a 21-gun salute. When this ruler died in 1855 he was succeeded by his son, Pertab Singh. British suzerainty came to an end in 1947.

Kashmir produced shawls which were outstandingly fine and light, a fact remarked upon by travellers from the West. In 1664 François Bernier, the first European to visit Kashmir, wrote of his amazement at the delicacy and softness of the local textiles (*Voyage dans les Etats du Grand Mogol*). These shawls were woven on handlooms by men, helped by young children and were about 1.80 m/71 in long by 1.20 m/47 in wide. The pines, or wide decorative borders at both ends of the shawl, were just under 30 cm/about 1 ft in height. In winter both men and women, Muslim and Hindu alike, wore them over their heads, draping them over the left shoulder like a cloak. Bernier observed that two types of shawl were made: one with local, very fine wool; the other with the soft underfleece hairs from the breast of the wild goat, the latter much more expensive. Bernier noted that he had never seen anything so exquisitely fine and it was a pity that they were often attacked by worms.

Some seventeenth-century miniatures provide us with a detailed portrait of a Moghul prince (see page 17) who is wearing a shawl which must have come from Kashmir; this makes one wonder when shawl weaving first began in Kashmir. According to Carl von Hügel (*Kaschmir und das Reich der Siek*), who visited Kashmir in 1836, the credit for starting the industry must go to Sultan Zayn al-Abidin, who in the fifteenth century summoned a highly skilled weaver named Naghz Beg from Turkestan to build a loom for weaving shawls. Four centuries later the weavers von Hügel wrote of still laid flowers on their revered guru's grave; shawl weaving had by then become one of Kashmir's main sources of income.

In winter the wild goats (*Capra hircus*) which are found on the high plateaux of Tibet and Central Asia grow a layer of soft down on their underbellies, beneath their normal coat of longer, coarser hairs: this underfleece helps them to survive extremes of cold at these high altitudes. When spring comes, the animals eliminate this extra layer of insulation by rubbing their bodies against bushes and rocks. The local inhabitants gather the fleece shed in this way and sell it in the Kashmir valley. Certain travellers who happened to witness this fleece "harvest" thought that the precious substance used in the weaving of shawls was a plant which grew like cotton. In other areas, including Kashmir itself, domesticated goats also produce an underfleece and are combed to remove it, but shawls woven with this wool are of inferior quality.

The raw material was sold and distributed among the Kashmiri women who picked out the kemp or coarse, rough hairs and sorted the fleece into two different qualities before spinning it on a spinning wheel. The superior fleece was reserved for the warp threads and for the finest shawls (being almost white it could be used just as it was or undergo dyeing to a light colour). The slightly coarser or greyish fleece was dyed and used for the weft.

Kashmiri weavers – always men – used a horizontal loom, two or three of them sitting side by side at the same loom. The women prepared the warps by "doubling" the thread, drawing it out while twisting it slightly. Then came the turn of the warpers, the men who put the warp into the loom: anything from 2,000 to 3,000 warp threads were necessary for a 1.20-m/47-in wide shawl. The vertical borders were woven on silk warp threads to give them more strength. The designer, known as the *naqqash*, decided on the pattern; the "colour caller," or *tarah-guru*, read the design from the bottom upwards and called out each colour in turn together with the number of warp threads under which the bobbin of weft had to pass. A pattern master, the *talim-guru*, then wrote these instructions down using the traditional signs or "shawl alphabet." The weavers kept this transcription (the *talim*) in front of them as they worked.

The technique used in the weaving of Kashmir shawls is similar to that used for the Gobelins type of tapestries: the decoration is formed by weft threads interlocked where the colours change, the weaver passing them between the warps using bobbins around which the variously coloured threads are wound. These shawls, however, differ from tapestry proper in their weave in that they are woven in 2/2 twill (see glossary). Working on the back (or reverse side) of the textile, the weavers interlock the coloured weft threads producing a slight ridge where the joins have been made: raised and two-coloured on the back but invisible on the right side (see page 186). This twill-tapestry or *espoliné* weave technique results in the border being stronger than the single colour field whose fragile, almost transparent material does not wear well and sometimes has to be completely replaced when damaged. Twill-tapestry (see glossary) can reproduce any design, in a very wide variety of colours, but is a very slow process. Two men would have to work at their loom for 18 months to make the average shawl, while a top-quality article would take three years. Until the early nineteenth century shawls were made in one piece. The warp threads had to remain stretched taut on the loom for the entire time it took to weave the shawl. Sometimes they broke, or the woven section was torn during the later stages of manufacture: this entailed the most incredibly meticulous repairs, known as "lost mending" since it had to be invisible from the right side. The men who performed this minutely detailed work were doomed to a total or partial loss of sight over the years. In order to help the warp threads to withstand the strain of being on the loom for so long, and to prevent them fraying, they were moistened at frequent intervals with a very thin rice flour paste; once the shawls were finished, they had to be washed to eliminate the starch and the resulting stiffness. "The best water," wrote Thomas Vigne, who travelled to Kashmir in 1840 or thereabouts, "is that of the canal which links the lake to the Drogjan lock. There is a round hole in the limestone blocks of the wash-house, measuring one and a half feet across and a foot in depth; the shawl is placed on the bottom and while water is poured on to it from above, it is trampled with bare feet for five minutes. A man takes it to the canal where he stands in the water and pulls it to and fro; he then slaps it hard against a flat stone. This last operation is repeated three or four times before the shawl is plunged into the canal water again. Finally, the shawl is set to dry in the shade (. . .) Something in the canal water gives these shawls their ineffable softness" (*Travels in Kashmir*).

Until the end of the eighteenth century these long shawls had a decorative border at both ends, the ornamentation consisting of a row of flowering plants or small pines on a natural unbleached or a coloured background. The Kashmiris also wove striped shawls and square ones decorated with medallions for the Turkish and Persian markets. A large part of the population was engaged in the industry whose products were exported all over the Middle and Near East. The British were the first European nation to develop an interest in the Kashmiris' woven goods, which reached them via the ships of the East India Company. Those ladies who could afford them found they subtly enhanced clothes which had a softer, more natural look to them than those of their French sisters whose sleeker lines betrayed the presence of whalebone corseting. During the last quarter of the eighteenth century British ladies took the Kashmir shawl to their hearts. In France only a few daringly chic individuals sensed the approach of a wind of change in customs and fashion and started to wear them. Among them was the Marquise de Sorcy de Thélusson, as can be seen from Jacques-Louis David's enchanting portrait of her, painted in 1790 (page 18). This painting is probably the first evidence of France's incipient passion for all things Oriental. Among the artists who have recorded details of cashmere shawls for us was Jean-Auguste-Dominique Ingres. When he was seventeen or nineteen (art historians are uncertain whether it was in 1797 or 1799), he sketched a young woman artist, Barbara Bansi, as she watched Garnerin's parachute jump. In one hand she is holding a small telescope and, more pertinently, has a light cashmere shawl of very simple design with one row of pines (page 20), draped about her. Until this period French women had been at a loss to know what to do with the exquisite shawls which their attentive menfolk brought home from their travels. When Napoleon's officers returned from the Egyptian campaign bearing gifts of these exotic weaves, their recipients were entranced by them. Fashionable ladies realized that nothing could be better suited to the new, classically inspired fashions than the softly draped folds of these shawls. Their discreet floral motif ornamentation added detail and interest to the sobriety of the plain textiles used for clothes at that time. These soft, swaying stoles also had the advantage of echoing arm movements, conferring particular grace on a dance which was, for this reason, called the dance "*du schall*" (to use the contemporary spelling in France around 1830–40).

Towards the end of the eighteenth century, the young and beautiful Lady Hamilton used to entertain her friends in their Neapolitan drawing rooms with theatrical displays, using cashmere shawls as props. Here is how the Comtesse de Boigne describes these entertainments in her *Mémoires*: ". . . her usual costume was a white tunic, gathered at the waist; her hair hung loose or was caught up with a comb (. . .) When she agreed to a performance, she would gather together two or three cashmere shawls, a large antique vase, an incense-burner, a lyre and a tambourine. With these few theatrical props, in her classical garb, she took up a position in the center of the drawing room. She would then throw over her head a shawl which reached right down to the ground and covered her completely and, hidden thus, draped the others about herself. The first shawl would then be lifted suddenly, sometimes she removed it altogether, sometimes only half removed it, so that it formed part of the draperies of the subject portrayed by her pose." Madame Vigée Le Brun also practised the art of draping shawls and used to compose *tableaux vivants* in St Petersburg during the years 1791–1800: "I used to choose the most handsome men and the most beautiful women for my models and draped them with some of the countless cashmere shawls at our disposal." Later she wrote to an English painter who, it seems, was no great admirer of her work: "It appears that you disapprove of my lace, but I have not painted any these fifteen years past. I far prefer shawls (. . .) Shawls really are a godsend for painters" (*Souvenirs*).

In France the craze for shawls spread like wildfire. Determined to emulate Josephine Bonaparte, the future empress, fashionable women had to have at least one shawl, and

Portrait of Sayyid Raju
Qattal.
India, Deccan school,
Golconda, late seventeenth
century (1680?).
Gouache, gold and silver on
paper, 24.5 × 16.2 cm/9½
× 6½ in.
Paris, Musée Guimet, Fonds
Musée Napoléon, N. 35667.

To protect himself from the
cold, this nobleman has
wrapped a small fur round
his neck and covered it with a
cashmere shawl. One of the
shawl borders is worn over
his left shoulder and down
his back, the other is thrown
forward over the same
shoulder. In the late
seventeenth century borders
were often decorated with a
very simple design of
flowering plants.

Jacques-Louis David
(1748–1825), *Portrait of the Marquise de Sorcy de Thélusson*, 1790.
Oil on canvas, 129 × 97 cm/51 × 38 in.
Sammlung der Bay. Hypoth. u. Wechselbank, Neue Pinakothek, Munich.

The marquise has a very attractive shawl draped around her shoulders, the borders of which are decorated with five rows of symmetrical pines. She was in advance of French fashion since the craze for shawls only took a firm hold eight or nine years later.

preferably several, as an accessory for their many gowns. In 1809 Baron Gros painted a full-length portrait of the Empress Josephine. She is shown wearing a dress made out of a long white cashmere shawl, its pine ornamentation enhancing the lower part of the skirt; a red shawl is wound round her waist, one end trailing on the ground like a train while the other end, draped forwards over her left shoulder, hangs down in front (page 24). Records show that Josephine owned about 60 shawls some of which had cost as much as 8,000–12,000 francs, an exorbitant price in those days. In spite of their being so expensive, demand for these shawls soon outstripped supply and the weavers of Kashmir had to change their production methods in order to increase their output.

From this time shawls were made in two pieces, on two looms. Once the two pieces had been woven, they were taken off the looms and joined together. A *rafugar*, or invisible mender, used a needle to join them together, picking up the loose warp threads of one unfinished edge and entering them into the corresponding section of the other half. Another method was to embroider the decoration rather than weave it into the shawl: the latter took three times as long as embroidering. The resulting lower price of these embroidered shawls amazed Europeans, who considered embroidery the height of artistry. *Espoliné* or twill-tapestry weave, a sort of embroidery on the loom, calls for infinitely greater accuracy. Any mistake made while embroidering with a needle can be unpicked and put right without it affecting the rest of the composition; the slightest error in twill-tapestry, however, has to be detected at once if it is to be corrected, otherwise all the subsequent weaving has to be undone. In Kashmir a shawl made a single piece, with twill-tapestry ornamentation, is called a *kanikar*; when the decoration is applied to a plain ground by embroidering with a needle, the shawl is known as *amlikar*. After 1810, the weavers compromised by making the shawls in two pieces, with twill-tapestry borders and the four corner ornaments embroidered with a needle.

From the early days of the First Empire a cashmere shawl was a suitable wedding gift from a bridegroom to his future wife, together with the more traditional jewels and lace. All this finery was exclusively reserved for married women and was considered inappropriate for a young, unmarried girl. Napoleon's wedding gifts to his second wife, Marie-Louise, included 17 shawls. From a watercolour by Benjamin Zix now in Cabinet des Dessins at the Louvre, we know that many of the aristocratic ladies who formed part of the Imperial couple's wedding procession in 1810, had a cashmere shawl carefully folded over one arm as they progressed through the Great Gallery of the Louvre.

The beginnings of European production

In spite of being so costly, shawls were increasingly sought after in Europe. Textile manufacturers both in Britain and in France sought to copy them, but envisaged a technique more in keeping with European traditions. In place of the silky soft goat's fleece they threaded silk warps on their drawlooms and wove shawls *au lancé*, passing the pattern weft from selvedge to selvedge (see glossary), using four or five colours for the weft, in wool, cotton and silk.

Weaving *au lancé* leaves the wefts free on the back of the cloth wherever they are not needed for the decoration on the right side. These floating threads on the wrong side were trimmed off once the shawl was completed in order to reduce its weight. Where decoration covers the entire surface area, an untrimmed shawl can weigh up to four times its trimmed weight. From the very first imitations and up to the end of the nineteenth century, European shawls with Kashmir ornamentation were, barring only a few exceptions, woven *au lancé* and trimmed. This technical characteristic is easily discernible by the uneven velvety texture of the back (page 186). The trimming process, however, weakened the shawl and thus, aesthetic considerations apart, European women tended to prefer Oriental shawls whose wefts were woven and interlocked, making their

Jean-Auguste-Dominique Ingres (1780–1867), *Barbara Bansi*, c. 1797.
Charcoal, stump and some white highlights on paper, 46.8 × 37.2 cm/18½ × 14½ in.
Paris, Musée du Louvre, Cabinet des Dessins, no. R.F. 11 684

In her left hand this young woman holds a telescope, through which she has just been able to observe Garnerin, the balloonist, make a parachute jump from a hot air balloon. The borders of her shawl are decorated with small pines.

Ingres often included cashmere shawls in his portraits of women, painted with such detail that they are not only beautiful but also valuable documentary evidence.

Parisian Fashions, plate no. 968, 1809.
Paris, Musée de la Mode et du Costume de la Ville de Paris.

A lady of fashion wearing a square shawl with medallions and stripes.

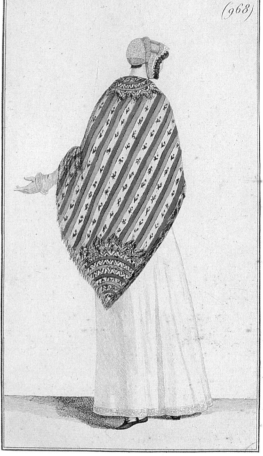

Louis-Leopold Boilly
(1761–1845), *The Downpour*
or *Paying to Cross*, 1805.
Oil on canvas, 32.5 × 40.5
cm/13 × 16 in.
Paris, Musée du Louvre.

This picture shows a family
caught in a heavy shower of
rain; they are walking along a
plank on wheels to avoid the
mud in the street. On the left
is a man whose job it is to
take payment for allowing
people to use the plank. The
young woman clutches her
most precious belongings:
her little dog, her purse and
her shawl.

Detail of the border of a long
shawl.
Kashmir, c. 1800. In around
1860 long shawls gave way to
square shawls.
Espoliné weave, 162 × 160
cm/64 × 63 in.
Paris, author's collection, no.
70.
Exhibited: Paris, 1982, cat.
no. 95.

With three rows of pines on
the border, this shawl looks
remarkably like the shawl in
Boilly's painting, above.

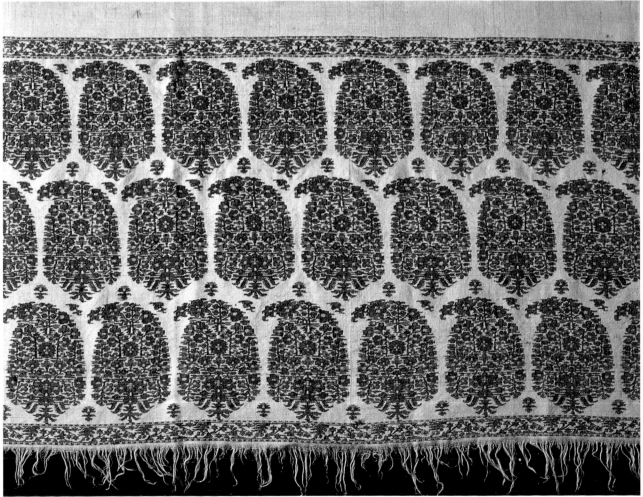

Opposite: Ingres, *Madame Rivière*, 1805.
Oil on canvas, 116 × 90 cm/45½ × 35½ in.
Paris, Musée du Louvre.

The pines on the border are much larger than in eighteenth-century shawls and still have a single colour background.

decorated sections much stronger. Early nineteenth-century European shawls were, moreover, woven in several pieces which had then to be sewn together: the two main borders, the two vertical borders and, finally, the plain field. In order to satisfy a less exclusive clientele, the Jouy factory of Oberkampf and the Mulhouse manufacturers started to produce printed "cashmere" shawls which were most attractive.

The French contribution

In 1806 Napoleon announced his Continental Blockade; goods which had been carried in British ships were to be prohibited from entering France (and other European countries). Since this inevitably applied to Indian textiles and shawls, the blockade proved a boon for the French silk industry which had been in decline since the Revolution and subsisted on orders from Napoleon's court. French manufacturers were quick to capitalize on the frustration felt by women who could now only acquire Kashmir shawls if they had been smuggled in or imported via Russia, at fabulous prices, and pitted their wits against each other in their efforts to produce imitation Oriental shawls. Production increased considerably. The most resourceful shawl manufacturer at the time of the First Empire was Guillaume Ternaux (1763–1833) who contrived to produce shawls of high quality. He had a factory in Rheims which specialized in shawls with white backgrounds, and another at Saint-Ouen, near Paris, which was renowned for its shawls with black grounds. Ternaux managed to import the special downy goat's fleece by way of Russia and tried to reproduce the Kashmirian twill-tapestry weave. He employed women and children to keep his labour costs low. While accepting that both the raw material (the goat's fleece) and the technique (twill-tapestry) of Kashmir's shawl industry outshone their European equivalents, Ternaux was determined to market shawls with a distinctively French look to them. Thus, in 1811 when the Minister of the Interior, Montalivet, placed an order with him for 12 shawls for the Court at the behest of

Anne Louis Girodet-Trioson (1767–1824), *The Indian*, 1807.
Oil on canvas, 145 × 113 cm/57 × 44½ in.
Montargis, Musée Girodet.

Six rows of pines decorate the border of this shawl.

They are of symmetrical design, like those on the shawl worn by the Marquise de Sorcy de Thélusson (page 18).

Detail of a striped long shawl. Kashmir, early nineteenth century. Twill-tapestry weave, 224 × 130 cm/88 × 51 in. Paris, A.E.D.T.A., no. 2292.

Most of the Kashmiri woven striped shawls were made for the Turkish and Persian markets.

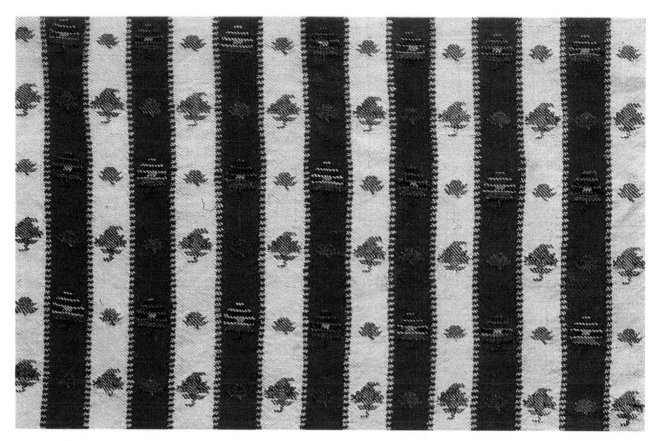

the chance to impress. During those 65 years, France's shawl manufacturers made periodic attempts to bring about the demise of the fantastical decorative schemes of Oriental shawls. The promotion of a distinctive French style would, they hoped, lead to the imported shawls which competed with their own products becoming outmoded, but they failed to convince women that Europe could outdo the East in artistry. It was this same European clientele, however, with its insatiable desire for change, which was to force the weavers of Kashmir to alter their traditional shawl designs.

The Jacquard loom

In April 1814 Napoleon was sent to Elba in exile. The monarchy was restored in the person of Louis XVIII, and many members of the aristocracy who had lived in exile during the First Empire returned to France. Protagonists and ethos changed but the backdrop remained the same. The Comtesse de Boigne wrote in 1814: "Having taken our leave of the Duc d'Angoulême, we stepped straight out into the *pavillon de Flore* which in those days was just a covered way, paved and open to the elements with no doors or windows, so we were as cold as if we were out in the street; one was not allowed to walk along through the palace rooms. This left us with a choice: we could either make our way through the underground kitchen passages and the outdoor galleries, or use our carriages to reach the *pavillon de Marsan*. The former entailed walking the whole way without one's shawl or pelisse since etiquette banned these from the château" (*Mémoires*). Shawls were obviously no longer considered formal attire. Ingres was still painting portraits of shawl-clad ladies in the early days of the Restoration but he was working in Rome, while David painted his *Ladies of Ghent* (oil on canvas, Paris, Louvre) with simple, unpretentious shawls around their shoulders. Isabey was alone in depicting three of his subjects in 1817 wearing five shawls between them at the top of the grand staircase in the Louvre: two ladies and a Persian gentleman, this last with no fewer than three draped

Ingres, *Madame Panckoucke*,
1811.
Oil on canvas, 93 × 68 cm/
36½ × 27in.
Paris, Musée du Louvre.

The coral red of Madame
Panckoucke's shawl matches
her jewellery and its design is
not unlike the pattern shown
on the opposite page.

about his person (page 33). The ladies could be almost anyone: wearing a Kashmir shawl was no longer out of the ordinary for prosperous people. François Couche's engraving entitled *A Lady is Given a Cashmere Shawl*, with IT IS FRENCH Woven into the Border (page 34), illustrates official disapproval of imported shawls.

French shawl manufacturers vied with each other in their endeavours to perfect their products. Spinners began to import the legendary goat's fleece from the high plateaux of Asia. In 1816 the first French shawls woven with pure cashmere warp and weft made their appearance, under the name of "French Kashmir shawls." Two years later, in 1818, Guillaume Ternaux financed an expedition to the East to bring some of the special goats back to France. Amédée Jaubert was put in charge of this mission (M. Tessier, *Mémoire sur l'Importation en France des Chèvres à Duvet de Cachemire*, Memorandum Concerning the Importation of Kashmir Goats into France) which ended in partial failure: of 1,289 goats, purchased from the Kirghiz tribesmen, only four hundred survived the journey. Moreover, France's temperate climate meant that the surviving goats produced so little of the downy underfleece that it was not worth rearing them. Undaunted, the ever-enterprising Ternaux crossed the shawl-goats with other breeds, one example among many of his tremendous entrepreneurial spirit. He was a true captain of industry, always prepared to take risks: he had realized how vital it was to mechanize, to trade on a global scale and to promote social progress. He was, however, too far ahead of his time and died impoverished in 1833. In belated recognition of his efforts the public dubbed the new shawls "Ternaux shawls."

In 1818 French weavers started to have the first Jacquard mechanisms fitted to their looms. Jacquard had presented his new invention to Napoleon in 1805. The mechanism was driven by a foot pedal worked by the weaver. This pedal drew forward a succession of punched cards, whose perforations ensured that the correct warp threads were lifted to weave the desired design. When the entire sequence of cards had been used, the set was run through again, resulting in a design repeat. Jacquard's invention did away with the need for a drawboy to pull the cords and raise the warp threads of the drawloom manually. It also enabled far larger designs to be woven. A leading authority on nineteenth-century weaving theory, Bezon, writes: "Not only did this admirable invention prove very helpful in the development of the shawl industry, but conversely most of the improvements made to the Jacquard mechanism as time went by were those deemed necessary by the manufacturers who used it" (*Dictionnaire Général des Tissus Anciens et Modernes*).

The development of decorative motifs

Without attempting to catalogue the benefits of the Jacquard process to weaving in general and to shawls in particular, it is worth noting its most significant effects. At the time of the First Empire, the pine-decorated main borders, the vertical borders and the plain field were woven separately and had to be sewn together. During the Restoration, French manufacturers first managed to weave their shawls in one piece on a silk warp, although the fringe gates and wool fringes had still to be woven separately and sewn on as shawl ends since silk fringes had a tell-tale sheen and sparseness, betraying the shawl's European provenance. Wool fringes gave the product the look of a "real" Kashmir shawl. From 1825 this was no longer necessary, as cashmere wool was henceforth imported for the warp threads. Shawls could now be made in one piece. It is worth remembering that the process was reversed during the nineteenth century in Kashmir, where shawls had been woven in a single piece for centuries.

The technical progress brought about by the introduction of the Jacquard loom, combined with the vistas opened up by the 1819 national exhibition of manufactured goods encouraged shawl manufacturers to create new designs: 1819 saw the first reference to a harlequin shawl. This was a long shawl, often with a white field, the border decorated by eight to ten pines in individual rectangular compartments, each of which had a different ground colour; the fringe was a continuation of the colour of each compartment's field. Multicoloured fringes made their appearance earlier in the form of striped shawls, but on a smaller scale. The small pines of the gallery were often harlequin as well, each contrasting with the pine below it (page 71). It is not known where the idea for this new type of shawl originated but it met with great success in France and in Britain where harlequin shawls were at their most popular in 1825. When the compartments of the borders were each to have a differently coloured field (the sequence might be red, blue, yellow, green and then start all over again with red) which would be at least 40 cm/15¾ in high, the relevant sections of the warp threads had to be dyed before weaving began. The length of warp threads, sufficient for at least six long shawls, were sent to the dyer. He then dyed the different bundles or hanks of warps to the weaver's requirements, having first tightly bound those sections which were not to be dyed. This prevented the various colours from seeping further up the threads, confining the colour to the

correct length. The warp was then sent back to the weaver where it was put into the loom and weaving could begin. This dyeing method meant that the compartments' backgrounds could be in unmixed colour. (French shawls were most frequently woven in 3/1 twill which meant that the weft of the ornamentation crossed over three warps, masking them, and then under one warp thread, leaving it visible: if there were any difference in shade between warp and weft, the background colour would not be solid.) It is interesting to note that this method of tie-dyeing, used by the silk industry in the eighteenth century and known as the "*chiné à la branche*" technique, was generally supplanted in 1816 by printing on the warp, a quicker and less laborious process. The shawl industry was almost alone in continuing with tie-dyeing for at least two thirds of the nineteenth century (M. F. Peyot, *Cours Complet de Fabrique pour les Etoffes de Soie*).

By the 1820s many shawls had already been in use for 20 years and were showing signs of wear, particularly in the plain field where

Detail of long shawl. France, 1811 (?). Twill-tapestry weave, wool, 274 × 146 cm/108 × 57½ in. Paris, private collection. Exhibited: Paris, 1982, cat. no. 28; Lyons, 1983, cat. no. 2.

The garland, which forms a border round the plain field, is made up of European flowers. Produced by Ternaux and still in the family collection, it may well have been woven at the same time as the set of 12 shawls delivered to the Emperor Napoleon in 1812.

Paris Fashions, plate no. 772, 1806.
Paris, Musée de la Mode et du Costume de la Ville de Paris.

The shawl is folded in such a way that the two pine-decorated borders cover the shoulders.

Paris Fashions, plate no. 1124, 1811.
Paris, Musée de la Mode et du Costume de la Ville de Paris.

This young woman is wearing a dress made out of a shawl, with another shawl to drape round her shoulders, reminiscent of the Empress Josephine's portrait on page 24, but here the colour scheme has been reversed.

Paris Fashions, plate no. 1175, 1811. Paris, Musée de la Mode et du Costume de la Ville de Paris.

The long shawl seems to have been folded in two, with both borders covering the model's left arm.

Paris Fashions, plate no. 2063, 1822. Paris, author's collection.

The pines on this shawl have lost their traditional shape and a "gallery" has been added above the inner horizontal border.

mending was far more obvious than in the
decorated sections. If the owner were to be able
to continue wearing the shawl this plain section
would have to be replaced by a newly woven
piece (when a change of colour might be wel-
come). Alternatively, the damaged section
could be discarded and the various borders
repositioned around the intact part of the field
and sewn back on again. As a result, many a
long shawl became square and the end borders
were then sewn on to adjacent sides to form a
right angle at one corner while the other two
sides were bordered by what had once been the
vertical borders, sewn on to the back. This
ingenious idea meant that when the shawl
could be folded almost in half, just short of the
middle or "hypothenuse" of these two differently bordered right triangles, both borders
would be on display. The result went under the
name of a *double-pointe* or turn-over shawl
(page 73). Several damaged long shawls could
be cut up and used to make one harlequin
shawl, so long as the pines from the salvaged
shawls were of approximately the same size.
Some women specialized in this work; they
concealed all the joins on the newly assembled
shawl by embroidering over them, even going
to the lengths of painting in any faded colours
with a brush.

Once the shawl had been woven it was handed over to the shearer or *tondeur* who trimmed
off the floating wefts; then it was the turn of the
dresser or *appreteur* who made sure that the
cloth had sufficient sheen and body to it. Both
these finishing processes were sometimes carried out by the same craftsman. This chain of
production had all begun, however, with the
designer. His was the truly creative role and
traditionally he was a permanent employee of
the manufacturer. Conversant with the prob-
lems inherent in the weaving process, he would
make allowances for the limitations of contemporary technology and the need to keep the cost
price as low as possible. During the Restoration
period, artists were recruited to shawl design.
The conception of art at the service of industry,
and therefore accessible to the masses, was an
altruistic one, and some artists responded to it,
the most famous being Amédée Couder

François Couche, *A Lady is given a Cashmere Shawl with IT IS FRENCH* woven into the border.
Engraving, c. 1815.
Paris, Bibliothèque Nationale, Cabinet des Estampes, n.Ef 215a, p. 23.

Once the Continental Blockade had been lifted, dealers were able to import shawls from India once more for their fashionable female clientele. Such competition threatened French manufacturers, who did their best to convince high ranking ladies to set a good example by buying French goods.

(1797–1864). In 1820 he founded a combined design studio and school to cover all aspects of industrial design for several industries: gold and silversmithing, cabinet making, wallpapers, carpets, shawls and silks. Many of the most outstanding industrial designers of the nineteenth century learned their craft in his *atelier*.

Couder designed for the Gobelins and Beauvais factories and was the first freelance designer. The work by which he set most store, his plans for public buildings: a Center of Arts and Industry and for a Royal Academy of Music, were never built. His shawl designs, however, were to earn him lasting fame. Some of these have survived; the earliest is for a long shawl, dated 1823 (page 65), on which the borders have ten harlequin pine compartments. A lattice of tiny branches and sprigs covers the whole of the white field, which has a medallion in its center and a harlequin gallery. This shawl painting is one of many in the collection of the Conservatoire National des Arts et Métiers in Paris, together with an explanatory note by Amédee Couder: "This design, which may today seem relatively plain was, at the time when it was made into a shawl, the last word in

magnificence. It was woven on a single Jacquard machine with one thousand hooks; both the warp and the weft, of the finest, purest cashmere wool, were plied yarn; in spite of being so richly figured all over with delicate motifs, the weave of the shawl was as fine as the best plain cashmere. It was made specially for the 1823 Exhibition by Pierre Fournel, a former artillery captain who had exchanged his sword for cashmere shawl manufacture . . ." (*Notices Explicatives*).

The national industrial exhibition was held at the Louvre from 25th August until 13th October, 1823; at that time we know the shawl was only half woven. It was completed a few days before Louis XVIII's death on 16th September, 1824. This means that it must have taken nearly two years to weave on a loom equipped with the Jacquard mechanism. If no other shawls were to be woven to this design, then its exorbitant price of 30,000 francs would seem to be justified.

In 1823 French shawl manufacturers were already exporting their goods. Ternaux even sold some in Asia. Travellers and designs made their way to and fro between Europe and the East. An English veterinary surgeon named Moorcroft brought back a set of eight very beautiful pine designs from Kashmir which are now in the Metropolitan Museum in New York. The general feeling at the time was that shawls from the Indian subcontinent had become a public necessity, along with coffee, tobacco, pepper and cinnamon. French dealers knew what their customers wanted and set off for Kashmir and the Punjab to order shawls from the weavers. They not only expressed preferences but sometimes went so far as to tell the weavers exactly what was required, prompting new ornamentation and influencing style in general.

French shawls had changed little since the beginning of the century although they were more richly decorated and their size had increased. The original ten pines on the borders had become nine or eight by the end of the Restoration but had grown taller. The space between the pines was occupied by sprigs and fillings. The vertical and horizontal borders

which surrounded the plain field had grown wider, from 2 cm/¾ in to 10 cm/4 in. In around 1810 corner ornaments started to appear in the four corners of the field. Five years later a gallery was added to the borders to form a double frame for the field; this was embellished by an extra gallery from 1825 onwards (see page 188 for key to the anatomy of a shawl).

In 1828 the botanist Victor Jacquemont was sent to India by the directors of the Jardin du Roi (now the Paris Natural History Museum). Born in 1810, he was to die of cholera in Bombay in 1832. While carrying out his assignment in India, Jacquemont kept a journal, later

published under the title *Voyage dans l'Inde*. His observations during the period starting in February 1831 are of particular interest to us: when he arrived at the Punjabi town of Ludhiana, he discovered the existence of a "Kashmir" shawl industry carried on by a colony of more than 1,000 Kasmiris, working 400 shawl looms. The prohibitive taxes levied in Kashmir at the time had forced these men to work outside their own country for a while. On page 185 of this book several extracts from Jacquemont's journal provide us with a considerable amount of detailed information on the lives of these shawl weavers. According to Jacquemont, the pines were anything from 70

36

cm/27½ in to 1 m/39½ in high; the smaller pines of the gallery were about 30 cm/11¾ in high; this means that the single colour field had shrunk considerably in size and must have measured only just over 1 m/39½ in square. For various reasons the shawls were woven in several pieces and some weighed a considerable amount.

In 1830 Charles X lost the French throne and was succeeded by Louis-Philippe, during whose reign commerce flourished as France caught up with industrialization. The shawl industry shared in this prosperity, not only in Paris but also in Lyons and Nîmes. The Jacquard mechanism meant that more shawls could be produced, in less time. The price of a standard quality shawl could now be afforded by a large number of women. At the same time a wealthy and ambitious middle class was swelling the ranks of the aristocracy and the numbers of elegant ladies. Even countrywomen wore shawls (as shown in the painting on page 36). Obviously there was a wide difference between the various qualities of shawl marketed: a range of smaller shawls which were not such luxury items as the long shawls with their pine decorations or the square shawls with large medallions, were sold at reasonable prices. Their modest ornamentation consisted of scattered flowers or small pines, or corner pines on a plain background, framed by a simple border. If a long shawl were torn or came apart it could be cut lengthwise in half, into two long scarves, or cut across the middle to make two nearly square shawls, each having only one deep border of pines: these were called *boîteux* or lop-sided shawls (page 68). These smaller items sold well and were often woven as such by the manufacturers; they sold for half the price of a complete long shawl. Long, narrow scarves were particularly popular in southern France where the warmer climate called for something less all-enveloping.

The raw materials also varied. The most expensive shawls were woven with pure cashmere warp and wefts; next down the scale were those with silk warp and wefts of cashmere or wool of varying fineness and quality. The real criterion when judging the quality of a French

shawl was how many different colours had been used for the weft. The number had a direct effect on the cost price. Good quality shawls were woven with seven colours. Less expensive shawls would have fewer than seven colours. Top-quality shawls, eight to fifteen.

Some Paris manufacturers hit upon the idea of a long shawl with hybrid decoration and patented it: one half had an ornamental gallery along three sides like a square shawl, the other half was decorated with large pines. Its owner could wear her shawl to show off its various facets on different occasions, so she effectively had three shawls in one. This proves that in 1847 the shawl industry was making every effort to tempt a less moneyed but far larger clientele (page 39).

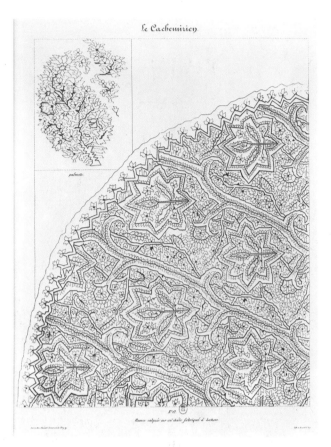

Right: *Medallion copied from a Shawl Woven in Lahore.*

Below: *Large Corner Ornament on Black Field, from a Shawl Produced in Kashmir.* These were plates 12 and 5 which appeared in Fleury Chavant's periodical *Album du Cachemirien*, Paris, 1837. Bibliothèque Nationale, Cabinet des Estampes.

These motifs, copied from Indian shawls and published in 1837, were intended as patterns for French shawl designers.

In 1837 the publishers Fleury Chavant brought out a magazine called *Le Cachemirien*, reproducing quantities of cashmere patterns which designers and manufacturers could consult for inspiration (page 38).

Shawl dealers sold their shawls in special white boxes with gold ties and the shop's name printed in gold letters. The boxes opened down the center by folding back both halves of the top; once closed the box was fastened by tying the cords. Ladies who owned one or more cashmere shawls could keep each one in its box but the done thing was to store them in a small wooden chest, purpose-made in fine wood. Edmond de Goncourt had just such a box in his bedroom: "I almost forgot to mention the marquetry box, made in the beautiful wavy, satiny sandalwood so sought after during the last century. This was where my elegant grandmother kept only the most beautiful of her cashmeres – she had so many of them . . ." (*La Maison d'un Artiste*).

The new fashions changed the outward female form: from 1820 waists gradually dropped to return to their rightful anatomical position; skirts grew slightly shorter, and fuller; the new leg-of-mutton sleeves, puffed out just below the shoulder, called for more bouffant hairstyles; more significantly, the new fashions were ill-suited to long shawls. The square shawl which had previously measured only about 140–50 cm/55–59 in square and was not considered an elegant accessory, was now to be worn on all occasions.

A great number of early nineteenth-century long shawls were cut up and remade into square shawls which were now embellished by rich decoration to underline their new status as high fashion accessories. The growth of the industry had made it possible to develop the Jacquard mechanism; wider decorative schemes could be produced without any sacrifice of quality of weave and design detail. The weavers could now work with fine, even and strong thread. A new type of shawl was launched on the market in the early 1830s: the quartered shawl, or *châle au quart*, where the design scheme (which could now be up to 90 cm/35½ in wide), fills a quarter of the shawl and is repeated on the other quarters.

It is therefore hardly surprising that several manufacturers submitted "rich" square shawls for the 1834 Exhibition. One manufacturer, Gaussen, wove a quartered shawl to a design by Amédée Couder who had called it the *Isfahan* shawl. Here the ornamentation, woven in ten colours, shows Persian-style buildings set against an emerald green background; the cupolas of the mosques are decorated with flags and point towards a central medallion. As part of the decorative scheme, cartouches enclose inscriptions in Arabic script. In the corners, the writing proclaims: "Entered for the Exhibition of French Manufactured Products, 1834," and on the cartouches arranged in a square in the center of the medallion: "Couder, 1834" and "Gaussen, 1834" (pages 78 and 79). In his *Notices Explicatives* the designer provides us with a commentary on his design and explanation is best left to him: "Before this design appeared, it was customary for designers to confine themselves exclusively to slavish imitations of Indian designs, including their most glaring imperfections. Amédée Couder was struck by this strange aberration and realized that the shortcomings of Indian shawls (such a striking exception to the usual elegant purity of all the other Eastern arts) must be due to the weavers' lack of skill and to the fact that they did not use the point papers [see glossary]. In addition to these two causes, their twill-tapestry weave [see glossary] gave an uneven outline to decorative motifs since the contours were blurred by the ridge and furrow of the twill. Repeated experiments confirmed his belief beyond any doubt and in 1834 he published a pamphlet on the subject. Seven years later, some pattern tracings arrived from Lahore which showed his comments to be fully justified. He then created this design, for which he chose the Persian style because of the elegance and smoothness of its curves. Having named the shawl after the capital of the country whence he had borrowed the style for his shawl, he then attempted to include as many motifs reminiscent of the East as possible: the choice of emerald green (the colour of the Emirs) for the background colour and a winged serpent

PARFAIT CHÂLE BREVETÉ

OU

TROIS CHALES EN UN.

Ce Châle se porte de trois manières différentes.

Nº 1. Châle Carré.

" 2. Châle Long à Grandes Palmes.

" 3. Châle Long uni seulement à Galeries.

CHAMPION & GERARD - FABRICANTS,

A PARIS, RUE Nº Sᵗ EUSTACHE, Nº 15.

39

Souvenir de L'Exposition des Produits de l'Industrie Française de 1839. Frontispiece of the album published in Paris, 1839, by Fleury Chavant. Paris, Bibliothèque Forney.

Eight double spreads of this album are devoted to "cashmere" shawls made in Paris. When staff at the Victoria and Albert Museum in London embarked on their study of French shawls, this album enabled them to identify two shawls in the museum's collection.

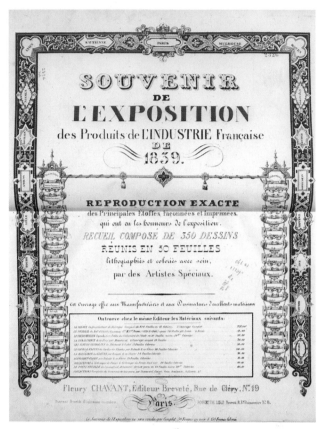

(part of Hindu iconography) enthroned in each corner on a sort of altar. The Sanskrit language was also represented by the name of the artist, the manufacturer and the date of production being inscribed in Oriental script; a profusion of plants suggested the luxuriant vegetation typical of Eastern climes, while the harmony and splendour of the colours used evoked the heady warmth of an empire from which enchantment emanated, the birthplace of many marvels."

There was certainly no trace of traditional Indian shawl ornamentation and, as Couder points out, the curves of the woven design had far smoother outlines when working out the design on point paper. The background, however, was not emerald green as originally planned, but allowed the red of the warp to show through. Red is the most usual choice for the colouring of the warp threads in the decorated section of a shawl since it shows off the flower motifs to best effect. The *Isfahan* shawl was woven with a red warp and a green weft for the ground, resulting in a shade verging on

bronze. European taste favours true colours, and although his shawl had been very well received the manufacturer, Gaussen, resolved to improve on this aspect next time. By the time the next exhibition opened, in 1839, he had remedied his mistakes, and exhibited a long shawl with a white background, called the *Nou-Rouz*, the original design of which bore Couder's signature (pages 83–88). In addition to buildings viewed in perspective, with realistic shadows, the designer had introduced men, women, animals and all sorts of plants and trees. Like the previous shawl, this was also quartered; the pattern had entailed the use of more than 100,000 punched cards and it was woven in 12 colours. Gaussen masked the red warp threads under the white wefts by using a special weave. The process was, however, very expensive. Since several copies of the *Nou-Rouz* shawls are extant, we know that the manufacturer amortized his costs by weaving at least four shawls to the same design.

Amédée Couder wrote of the *Nou-Rouz*: "Although the description posted below this shawl appears to make further explanation superfluous, we think that it may prove helpful to say a few more words on the subject. The *Nou-Rouz* is Persia's most important festival, being at one and the same time the Festival of the Flowers and the first day of their New Year: in the East they are undoubtedly more logical than we Westerners, for they start their new year when nature reawakens. In the middle of this shawl the shah is shown mounted on a white elephant, surrounded by the dignitaries of his empire, receiving homage from vassal states. Another part of the decor shows his kingdom's book of civil and religious laws lying open on a sort of altar. A long procession has formed, with deputations laden with costly gifts and, perhaps, tax revenue from the various provinces, slowly wending their way towards their powerful sovereign underneath triumphal arches which have been erected to mark the arrival of spring and the overall spirit of celebration. This magnificent caravan takes the place of the gallery; the border shows the interior of the palace: through one archway we glimpse a splendid feast, in another a sensuous

41

contours of their patterns acquired elegance and minutely studied details; it seemed fitting that they should now set the Indians themselves on the road to progress by sending them spirited new designs, full of sweeping lines and fresh colours. They proved receptive and quick to learn, willing to prove that in future they would be able to dispense with our designs, spurred on by a noble pride in their craft. If proof were needed, one has only to take a look at the very beautiful shawls created entirely without our help and which we are now importing from them."

Shawls of this type with their realistic, figurative style, bereft of any imitation of Kashmir ornamentation, are known as renaissance shawls. It is easy to understand why French manufacturers felt that at long last they were no longer the pupils of Eastern master craftsmen once they had created these revolutionary new designs. Although the fashion for renaissance shawls had soon passed and the industry reverted to the imitation of Indian products, nevertheless it had a lasting effect on shawl decoration, which from then onwards was a synthesis of pines and architectural motifs. Couder also points out that Indian designs already echoed some of the more graceful, curving contours created by French artists.

Another manufacturer, Bournhonet who had taken over Ternaux's business, had a long shawl on view at the 1839 exhibition. It had been designed by Hérault & Léon and featured Gothic architectural motifs with long, serrated pines crossing over them. The maker had found the simplest solution to the problem of obtaining a solid colour background: in at least one of the shawls woven to this design the ground is red (pages 80 and 81).

The revolution in style heralded by the renaissance shawls led to other changes. Fine quality shawls now began to have harlequin fringe gates; this was nothing new for striped and harlequin shawls, where it was inherent in the design. Now, however, harlequin fringe gates were to be the norm for all top-quality shawls, regardless of the ornamentation of the border; the fringe gates altered gradually between 1834 and 1870 and these changes

dancing display. The *Isfahan* shawl and its *Nou-Rouz* successor triggered a dramatic change in the shawl industry, resulting in what came to be known as the "renaissance" style which lasted for several years. This genre signalled the disappearance of any surviving traces of the traditional Kashmir motifs, especially the heavier, irregular shapes: contemporary taste favoured very graceful, clear-cut outlines. The fickleness of fashion brought its inevitable reaction, however, and imitation of Indian shawls was soon desirable once more. But this "renaissance" had given French designers a chance to display greater resourcefulness and skill; others now looked to them for the inspiration they had once sought elsewhere. The well-rounded

Cashmere Shawl Made by Frédéric Hébert & Co., Paris, plate no. 4 from the *Souvenir de l'Exposition des Produits de l'Industrie Française de 1839.* Paris, Bibliothèque Forney.

Border of pines for a long shawl. Two confronted pines and part of one adorsed pine, marked only by outlines, are superimposed on a complex design of flowers, leaves and creepers.

provide a rough guide to the dating of shawls (see page 189).

Long shawls came back into vogue around 1839 after being out of fashion for a while, for by then sleeves were fuller further down the arm, closer to the wrists, while skirts grew longer once more. In the album *Souvenir de l'Exposition de 1839* an equal number of square and long shawls are shown. The designer of one of the latter probably drew on an Indian shawl for inspiration. The classic decorative scheme is retained: large pines on the border and a gallery of smaller pines surrounding the field. But these large and small pines do not all face the same way, they are arranged back to back or facing one another. Renaissance shawls had already discarded the inner horizontal border that had previously separated the large pines from the gallery. The new shawls only retained the vertical and outer horizontal borders to provide a frame. After 1840 Indian-style shawls gradually lost this inner horizontal border. Sometimes it was retained in the form of arches over the pines (page 112), sometimes the pines and their attendant scrolls crossed over the inner horizontal border, partially hiding it, and occasionally this border was pushed higher, encroaching further on the field, to make room for ever-larger pines, giving the effect of a bar across the shoulders when the shawl was worn by its fashionable owner. This was not popular, however, and the inner border disappeared before 1850.

By 1836 or thereabouts pines of all sizes had encroached on the field of Kashmirian shawls. Ornamentation grew ever more profuse and the shawls increasingly heavy to wear. Carl von Hügel, who was in Kashmir at that time, thought they were really more like carpets, made for the Persian and European markets, for they were no longer worn in India. The deep border sported two rows of pines, only leaving room for a much smaller field. The most popular shawls were those which were copies of English imitations. Von Hügel describes a workshop in Kashmir: "Twenty-four weavers work at eleven looms in the following way:

2 looms with 3 weavers each for the large pines
4 looms with 2 weavers each for the small pines
1 loom with 2 weavers for the field
4 looms with 2 adolescent weavers each for the borders

"Each of the very best shawls is made up of fifteen pieces. Two shawls are always woven at the same time. Looms weaving the same pattern are worked simultaneously; one of the weavers who is thoroughly familiar with the

43

design recites each step for his fellow workers. These twenty-four weavers will take from six months to a year to complete a pair of shawls. *Jamewar* (gown pieces), or striped weaves, are about 2.65 m [8 ft] long and 1 m [39½ in] wide and are woven in four pieces; the Indians wear them over their tunics in winter, but never as turbans nor over their shoulders as a shawl. Plain materials woven in pashmina (cashmere) are produced in the Punjab and in Hindustan by emigré weavers. In the days of the Mogul emperors there were 40,000 looms each worked by an average of three weavers, making a total of 120,000 weavers in Kashmir. Under Afghan rule there were still 23,000. Nowadays [1836], there are only 2,000, 1,000 of whom specialize in long and square shawls, 600 in *jamewar* and 400 are engaged in weaving plain shawls or Kashmir material. These weavers produce a total of 3,000 shawls and pieces of material, and 1,200 *jamewar* each year" (*Kaschmir und das Reich der Siek*).

There were many causes for the decline in the numbers of weavers in Kashmir. The principal one was the exorbitant taxes imposed by the Sikhs which forced the weavers to leave their native country. Then there were the recurrent famines and cholera epidemics which ravaged Kashmir. Another reason was simply that the milder climate of the Punjab was more congenial and the weavers found they did not need to spend so much to eat, clothe themselves and keep warm. Expatriate weavers settled in Nurpur, Jommlu, Amritsar, Ludhiana and even Delhi. But, as Bernier had already commented in the seventeenth century, the most beautiful shawls of all were made in Kashmir: the workforce and the raw materials could be moved to another country but Kashmir's pure air and incomparable water were irreplaceable. The properties of water have an effect on how dyes take and on the washing of the shawls, when they should become very soft. Once Kashmiri shawls had been washed they were taken to a government official who affixed his stamp, the size of a man's hand, to them in return for a payment which varied according to the value of the shawl. Anyone found in possession of a shawl which did not have this seal was liable to a fine; when a shawl was washed after use the stamp disappeared and the official would stamp it again, this time free of charge.

In addition to these and other reasons for the decline of the shawl industry in Kashmir, von Hügel mentions the unpopularity of Indian shawls in Europe and the fact that even the Indians themselves were beginning to express a preference for English shawls. In 1872, when William Cross addressed a Scottish audience, he told them that the Franco-Indian style had exerted great influence on the Paisley shawl-making industry from 1842 onwards. Both men and designs were travelling further than ever before.

The "signed shawl"

The designer who had the greatest influence on the last 30 years of the great age of shawl production, was Antony Berrus (1815–83.) Having studied at the Ecole de Dessin in Nîmes, where he was born, he became resident designer at a carpet factory. He later worked for a shawl manufacturer in Nîmes who moved his factory to Lyons in 1838 and Berrus became his business partner. Berrus finally founded his own company in Paris, leaving the management of day-to-day affairs to his brother Emile. The two brothers predictibly traded under the name of Berrus Frères and met with enormous success: towards the end of its existence the company employed nearly 200 designers. Berrus designs were sold to manufacturers in Paris, Lyons and Nîmes as well as to the Scottish and Austrian shawl industries, and were even bought by shawl makers in the Kashmir valley. Berrus was the creator of the most widely successful French cashmere style. His designs were not, however, bought by the most famous shawl manufacturers who kept to their traditional practice of having a designer among their permanent employees. This meant that Berrus's dazzlingly accomplished shawl designs never took shape on the looms of the great masters of the craft.

Following the abdication of King Louis-Philippe, Prince Louis Napoleon was elected President of the Republic in 1848 and proclaimed Emperor of France four years later.

Reversible square shawl.
Lyons (?), c. 1849.
Double cloth, silk, 182 ×
182 cm/71½ × 71½ in.
Lyons, Musée Historique
des Tissus, no. 40350.
Exhibited: Paris, 1982, cat.
no. 119; Lyons, 1983, cat.
no. 44.

The ground on one side of
this shawl is black, and green
on the other. Both are
figured with luxuriant
foliage. Lyons was the capital
of the silk industry in
nineteenth-century France
and was famous for its
shawls, which were exported
as far afield as South
America. The Victoria and
Albert Museum in London
has a shawl with identical
figured motifs but in
different colours in its
collection (no. T. 171.1978).

Opposite: Alfred Stevens (1823–1906), *Do You Want to Come Out With Me, Fido?*, 1859.
Oil on canvas, 61.5 × 491 cm/24 × 19 in.
Philadelphia, Philadelphia Museum of Art,
W.P. Wilstach collection.

The long shawl which the young woman has thrown over her shoulders to keep her warm during her walk can be compared with the shawl shown on this page. It has the same decoration of S-shaped pines on a black central ground.

Detail of long shawl. Northwest India, c. 1855–60. Twill-tapestry, woven in several pieces which were then cut and sewn together, cashmere, 321 × 138 cm/ 126 × 54 in.
Paris, author's collection, no. 53.
Exhibited: Paris, 1982, cat. no. 90.

A tree of life in the center is flanked by two tall pines. The coloured squares above the fringe are decorated with *mihrab* (niches in the inner walls of mosques to indicate the direction of Mecca); these are woven and not embroidered, unlike most Indian shawls. A shawl of identical design is to be found in the Yale University Art Gallery, where it was exhibited in 1975, cat. no. 21.

During this turbulent time another exhibition was held, in 1849, at which a new type of shawl made its mark: the *châle végétal*. This style provided the inspiration for a number of Berrus's most accomplished extant designs. Waving pines stretch up towards the center among luxuriant flowering branches and ferns. Sometimes the elongated pines turn into a palm tree, with a typical scaled trunk and its apex transformed into a treetop. This wealth of exotic and imaginary vegetation sometimes sheltered wildlife: snakes, salamanders and butterflies, with birds of paradise on the wing in pursuit of insects. The only surviving shawl of this type known to the author (illustrated on page 114) is woven in 12 colours, a sure sign of its rarity.

Shawls with plant forms remained in vogue until 1851. Carnations, dahlias and irises were discernible in some of the designs, proof of the Oriental style's disfavour: in some shawls only the framing borders and the harlequin shawl gates survived. Plant-decorated shawls were also made in silk, both long and square, and the latter were sometimes reversible (page 45). These reversible shawls called for a far more intricate weave: there were no floating wefts to be trimmed, so that they did not have to be folded in half to hide the back; Lyons was the production center, exporting to Britain and South America. The wider, crinoline-supported skirts of the Second Empire brought square shawls back into fashion.

In 1844 Paul Godefroy, a shawl manufacturer and textile printer, invented a technique for colour printing the warp to match the outlines of the design to be woven; his remarkable achievement meant that some shawls were now made with their center section divided into compartments with different ground colours, the ornamentation was the same but the fields were woven with different colour wefts (pages 109, 124 and 125).

Pivoting designs (*châles à pivot*) made their first appearance at the same time as the plant-decorated shawls. Similar in style, the difference lay in the disposition of the decoration, with only one design repeat. Once half the shawl had been woven, this one design was swivelled through 180 degrees around a central point. This gave a diagonal effect (pages 107, 120). Several of the most outstanding manufacturers produced pivoting shawls and put them on show at the exhibitions which became international from 1851 onwards. Berrus excelled in this type.

The Great Exhibition of 1851 was held in London, at the Crystal Palace. Manufacturers from both sides of the Channel exhibited some breathtaking products. Couder sent one of his shawl designs while Berrus sent at least three, one of which showed cupola-topped buildings emerging from luxuriant vegetation intertwined with palmes, in a blue-shaded fantasy world.

This orgy of creative imagination was accompanied by a surge in the development of trade and industry, posing a threat to shawl manufacturers. They now had to contend with "counterfeit" shawls. Biétry, a former spinner turned cashmere shawl producer, published a pamphlet in 1849 in which he asked other manufacturers to mark their products. He also inveighed against the unfair competition of shawls sold as cashmere products when they were actually made of cotton or mixtures of silk waste and wool. Responding to this invitation to sign and guarantee their work, some shawl makers wove their initials into the left-hand corners of the harlequin borders. Biétry himself wove the word *cachemire* into the right-hand corner of some of his shawls (page 184). He also sewed round labels bearing his name and guaranteeing the cashmere content to the reverse side of some of his less expensive shawls. Other shawl makers followed his example. Frédéric Hébert wove an H followed by the words *Cachemire Pur* into the central field of his shawls in wool of contrasting colour (page 111).

At the next exhibition, which was held in Paris in 1855, Berrus displayed another of his innovations: the coats of arms of his royal customers were woven into the corners of harlequin shawl ends reminiscent of the practice of tapestry manufacture. In this case the arms of the Emperor Napoleon III appeared on a pivoting shawl. Reporting on the industrial

Claude Monet (1840–1926), *Madame Gaudibert, Wife of a Le Havre Shipowner,* 1868. Oil on canvas, 217 × 138.5 cm/85½ × 54½ in. Paris, Musée d'Orsay.

Madame Gaudibert is wearing a square Indian shawl in which small pieces have been sewn together, with fringing on all four edges. It is the same type as that shown on pages 176 and 177. This is one of the last paintings to show an elegant woman in a cashmere shawl. From 1869 onwards the wearing of a bustle made shawls look ungainly.

Hindus weaving shawls, giving a demonstration of their work at the Great Paris Exhibition of 1878. This engraving appeared on July 13, 1878 in issue no. 15 of the *L'Exposition de Paris*. Paris, author's collection.

The Indian standing by the loom weaves narrow strips which are then cut out and sewn together by his fellow craftsman. The resulting shawls tended to be heavy and rather coarse.

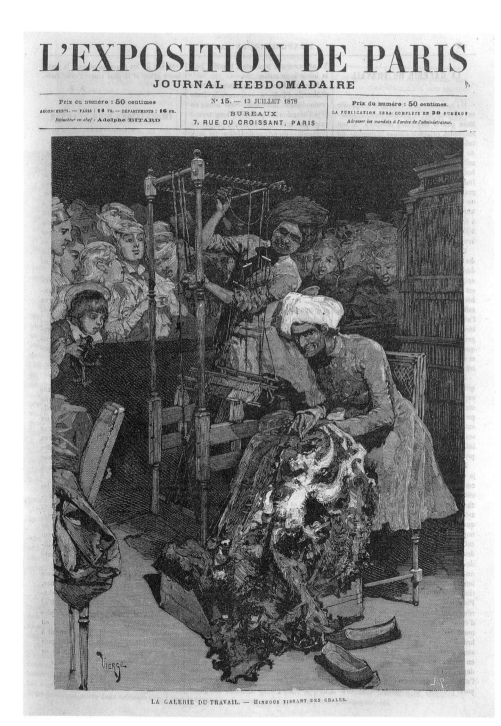

L'EXPOSITION DE PARIS
JOURNAL HEBDOMADAIRE

Prix du numéro : 50 centimes.   N° 15. — 13 JUILLET 1878   Prix du numéro : 50 centimes.

ABONNEMENTS. — PARIS : 14 FR. — DÉPARTEMENTS : 16 FR.   BUREAUX   LA PUBLICATION SERA COMPLÈTE EN 30 NUMÉROS

Rédacteur en chef : Adolphe BITARD   7, RUE DU CROISSANT, PARIS   Adresser les mandats à l'ordre de l'administrateur.

LA GALERIE DU TRAVAIL. — HINDOUS TISSANT DES CHALES.

designs at this exhibition, a journalist did in fact note that the Empress Eugénie had ordered a Berrus design, to be woven by Biétry. But there is no proof that this was the shawl in question. The shawl shown on pages 127–31 is the same as Berrus's design on page 126 except for the lower center section, and has the British Sovereign's coat of arms and mottoes in the corners: *Honi soit qui mal y pense, Dieu et mon droit*. The shawl shown on page 138 has the inscription *Paris Exposition 1855* woven into the corners (page 184).

Subsequently manufacturers found it cheaper to affix a gilt seal to their shawls. This bore their initials, the cross of the Legion of Honour if this had been awarded to them, and a list of their exhibition medals and prizes. Their practice of imitating the signatures of Indian shawls by weaving signs into the small central field has proved frustrating as they have yet to be deciphered. In 1855 square shawls without a plain central field were also in vogue (page 142). Designs featuring architectural motifs were in evidence as well. The shawl bearing the Royal Coat of Arms had separate pines, set in *mihrabs* as if they were sacred objects; one design evokes the rococo style of the eighteenth century; another shows a round tent in the middle of a Persian garden flanked by small pagodas. An Englishman described the French shawl exhibits and exhorted manufacturers in his own country to emulate them but without copying their less felicitous details: "Here are Chinese temples to decorate the back of a lady!" (G. Wallis, *The Exhibition of Art-Industry in Paris*, 1855.) Paisley and some American museums have chinoiserie shawls in their collections: the French examples very probably date from 1855. These shawls were outstanding pieces of craftsmanship but were not really wearable.

In 1857, when E. F. Hébert had not long taken over his father's shawl business, he wrote a monograph on the life of a Parisian shawl weaver, published by F. Le Play 30 years later. Further advances in technology made it possible to reduce the number of shuttles used: this was known as the *mariage des couleurs* or "marriage of colours" and was invented in 1849. If orange was required, a red weft and a yellow weft were passed through the same shed; for dark red, one red warp and one black warp were used together, etc. Another sign of progress, dating from 1856 was the introduction of chemical dyes to take the place of vegetable and mineral dyes. This was one of the causes of the sameness of shawl colours after 1860.

At this point crinolines grew longer at the back, forming a sort of train which made a good display platform for long shawls. Gonelle Frères' design studio introduced "burnous" shawls (see glossary) which were worn like capes. A design for one of these shawls is shown on page 148, and three contemporary photographs on page 149, making the wearer look rather dumpy to twentieth-century eyes. Unfortunately too few women had the grace of Alfred Stevens's model (page 47). She is shown wearing an Indian shawl with a small S-shaped pine in each corner of the field, similar to those of the shawl on page 46.

The member of the jury reporting on the shawl section of the Great Exhibition in London in 1862 was the elder son of Gaussen, the manufacturer of the *Isfahan* and *Nou-Rouz* shawls. He notes that "examples of the two schools which have always provided inspiration for French shawl designers were represented: the Indian school, with M. F. Hébert, jr. as its leader and the *fantaisiste* or fantasy school, the best exponents of which were the house of Duché, A. Duché the younger and Brière & Company"; he goes on to say "the Indian style is particularly suited to the home market and the fantasy style for export." As to Berrus, it seems that his prolific output appealed to devotees of both schools. He sent numerous designs to the exhibition, shawl designs painted in gouache, and pen and ink drawings on tracing paper. One of these drawings shows a crowned female figure, enthroned above shawl draperies; various styles are represented: narrow pine-decorated borders; large pines; scattered smaller pines; and a shawl with plant forms. Perhaps this display was a homage to Queen Victoria (page 147).

A close look at the Berrus designs of 1862–74 shows that they are still full of flair, but the

Detail of woven strip with motifs ready to be cut out. Northwest India, last third of nineteenth century. Twill-tapestry weave, cashmere. Paris, Musée de l'Homme, Département d'Asie, no. X 46.5. Exhibited: Paris, 1982, cat. no. 174.

Once cut out, these motifs would be sewn up to make a shawl as shown on the opposite page.

imagination so much in evidence during the preceding 15 years has started to grow stale. There are endless variations on the theme of two pines or two pairs of pines, extremely elongated with a backdrop of hackneyed Oriental designs. Detail changes do occur: around 1862 the Greek key-pattern is sometimes displayed, giving way in 1867 to festoons and to a white edging which picks out the outlines of the ornamentation.

Large numbers of shawls were produced at this time and many of them have survived, showing little variation in their colourings. Early chemical dyes were crude, and faded when exposed to light. These brownish-red shawls differ only in design. Industrial advances meant that machines, driven by steam or electricity produced increasingly regular weaves without any human intervention save in an emergency; output had increased dramatically but the penalty was the absence of any individual touches made as weaving progressed, such as the colour changes which make the oldest cashmeres so enchanting. Large shawls grew cheaper, bringing them within reach of the rural population, among whom they remained popular until the end of the century. A young married countrywoman would wear a cashmere shawl over her black wedding dress; later on she would wrap her baby in it to keep the child warm by the font when it was baptized. Manufacturers could therefore turn out the same patterns year after year. The large shawl design by Charles Sevray (page 53), shown at the 1878 Exhibition was probably the last. This exhibition took place at the Champ de Mars in Paris and India sent two craftsmen to demonstrate how shawls were made in their native country (see illustration on page 50). One man is weaving a narrow band of patterns on his loom for his fellow worker to cut out then sew up like a patchwork, joining the small ornamental motifs together to make a decorated shawl which was called a *tilikar* (pages 176 and 177).

From 1860 onwards, as European shawls dropped in price, Indian weavers were forced to increase their output. Shawls woven at speed were coarse and heavy. Western customers lost interest in Indian shawls and soon European shawls were also out of favour, mass production having robbed them of their prestige. From about 1869, when fashion took to bustles to accentuate the curve of the back, women could no longer dream of wearing shawls.

The political and economic vicissitudes caused by the Franco-Prussian War of 1870–71, ending in defeat for the French, meant that the shawl industry in the Indian subcontinent found itself without this export market; the weavers had no work and many died in the famine of 1877. Although the fashion for shawls had passed, it remained customary for a few more years for a ritual French cashmere to be included among wedding gifts. Smart newly married women kept them in their boxes and never wore them. This is why shawls of this period are sometimes still as good as new. Towards the end of the nineteenth century they were used as wall hangings or as a covering for the piano. Older, worn shawls were cut up and made into *visites* or waisted jackets, the skirt slit behind so that they hugged the curve of the back; these jackets were lavishly braided to match the colours of the shawl material.

The vogue for cashmere shawls had created flourishing industries in Britain and France but lasted less than a century during which the soft, light and discreetly decorated early weaves had gradually changed into over-ornate, heavy shawl-rugs; the central field had shrunk with the encroachment of giant pines until it was just a small black square.

Textile and embroidery designers have never completely dropped the pine motif: it keeps reappearing every now and then. Kashmir shawls have had no place in women's wardrobes for many decades but during the past few years printed shawls and long scarves have revived the nineteenth century's alternative to the genuine article. Another generation is now able to appreciate the rich and strange patterns of a decorative style which lends itself to endless improvisation and variation. Perhaps this book may lead to fresh interpretations of an old and magnificent art.

Designs and shawls in European collections

On the previous page: design for a long shawl by Charles Sevray, 1878. Gouache on paper, 86 × 79 cm/34 × 31 in. Paris, Musée National des Techniques, C.N.A.M., no. 13,739.

It is not known whether a shawl was actually woven to this design. Perhaps it was destined only to be a shawl designer's nostalgic farewell to an art which, he knew, was already doomed by the onward march of fashion.

Long shawl (fragment) with pine-decorated border. Kashmir, last quarter of the eighteenth century. Twill-tapestry weave, cashmere, 23 × 86 cm/9 × 34 in.

Paris, A.E.D.T.A., no. 1599. The pines enclose a small vase which in turn contains flowering stems and large flowers. A serrated leaf is shown on either side of the vase, springing from a footed dish.

51

Fragment of a long shawl, detail of border motif. Kashmir, last quarter of the eighteenth century. Twill-tapestry weave, cashmere, 19 × 126 cm/ 7½ × 49½ in. Paris, A.E.D.T.A., no. 1436.

A similar motif to that shown on the opposite page: a dish and two curving lateral leaves, in the middle of which is a small vase containing the bouquet. The flowers and stems are even more luxuriant than in the previous fragment. The pines on these two relatively rare examples of late eighteenth-century borders are no higher than 20 cm/8 in and contrast against the plain ground.

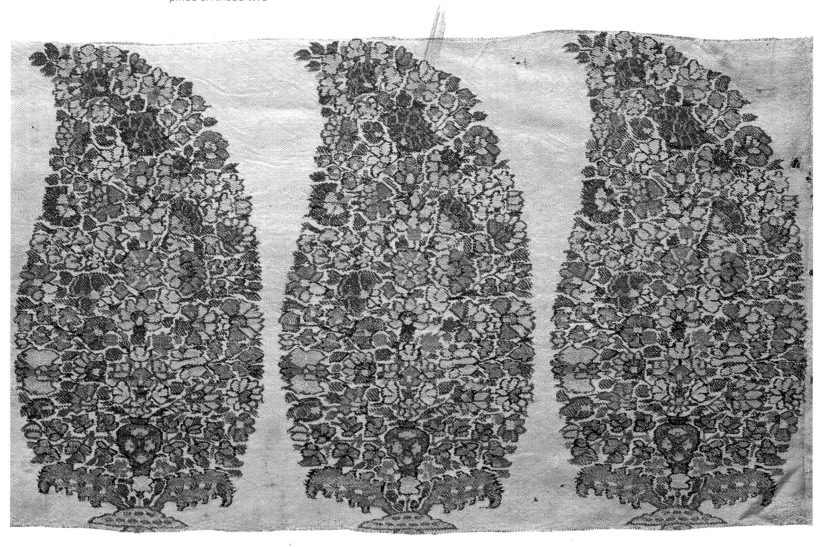

Opposite: detail of long shawl; border decorated with small pines. Kashmir, late eighteenth century.
Twill-tapestry weave, cashmere, 336 × 130 cm/ 132 × 51 in.
Paris, A.E.D.T.A., no. 291.
Exhibited: Paris, 1982, cat. no. 1.

Note the almost transparent quality of the fabric.

Fragment of a long shawl with pine-decorated border.
Kashmir, early nineteenth century.
Twill-tapestry weave, cashmere, 37 × 136 cm/ 14½ × 53½ in.
Paris, A.E.D.T.A., no. 2044.

A large flower forms the apex of each pine; the latter are taller than the earlier examples (31 cm/ 12 in high) and the space between them is filled with a flowering branch by the apices and small bunches of flowers below. There are two thick roots at the base of each bouquet.

Detail of long shawl, its border decorated by eight pines.
Kashmir, 1815 (?).
The borders are woven in twill-tapestry, cashmere, the corner ornaments embroidered, 304 × 135 cm/9 ft 11½ in × 53 in.
Paris, Musée National des Techniques, C.N.A.M., no. 9528.
Exhibited: Paris, 1982, cat. no. 15.

This shawl was woven in two halves, joined by a seam which is invisible from the right side; the numerals, 1, 8, 1, 5 are legible in the center of a circular stamp on the white field. The pine has two sections, the larger outer pine enclosing a smaller one, which in turn contains yet one more, rather like a Russian doll.

Long shawl with borders decorated by nine pines (detail).
Kashmir, 1810–20. Twill-tapestry weave, cashmere, the vertical borders are sewn on, 284.5 × 132 cm/112 × 52 in.
Paris, A.E.D.T.A., no. 1359.

In addition to the parrots roosting among the flowers, there is also a horseman shown at the edge of the corner ornament. During the 1820s, spaces between pines were filled and the main and vertical borders grew broader.

On pages 60–61: detail of long striped shawl. Kashmir, first third of the nineteenth century. Twill-tapestry weave, cashmere, 224 × 92 cm/ 88 × 36 in. Paris, A.E.D.T.A., no. 2191.

On this page: detail of long shawl, the border containing eight pines. France, 1810–20. Woven *au lancé*, trimmed on back, silk and cotton; the borders and the ground were woven separately, 302 × 135 cm/ 119 in × 53 in. Paris, author's collection, no. 3. Exhibited: Paris, 1982, cat. no. 22.

The plant forms have become increasingly stylized; the vertical and horizontal borders have gradually widened. The "sectioned" effect of the pines is very distinct. During the period 1810–20 either four corner ornaments or a small gallery appeared on the plain ground; only rarely were both used together.

Long shawl with seven pines on the border, (detail).
France, c. 1820.
Woven *au lancé*, trimmed on back, silk, cotton and wool; the fringes have been sewn on separately, 248 × 126 cm/ 97½ × 49½ in.
Paris, author's collection, no. 4.
Exhibited: Paris, 1982, cat. no. 39.

Made by a craftsman rather than one of the major manufacturers; the gallery and the corner ornament now differ somewhat from Oriental styles. Note the ribbon tied round the bunch of flowers of the corner ornament.

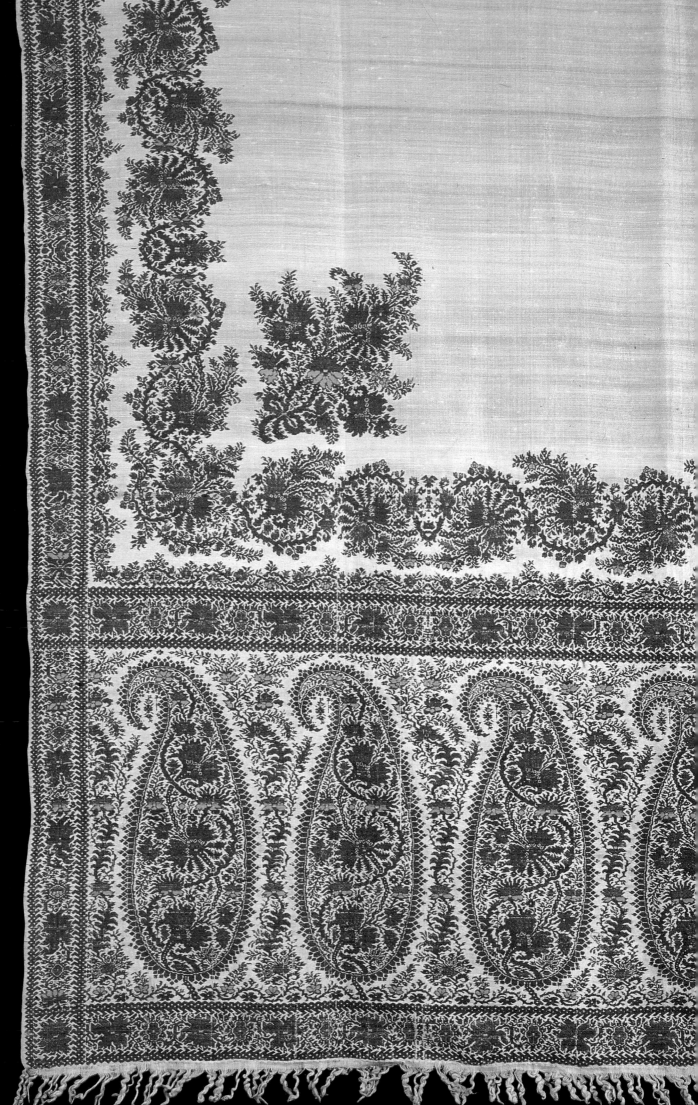

Design for a harlequin shawl, signed Amédée Couder, Paris, 1823. Gouache on paper, 65.6 × 32 cm/26 × 12½ in. Paris, Musée National des Techniques, C.N.A.M., no. 10.332.
Exhibited: Paris, 1982, cat. no. 85a; Lyons, 1983, cat. no. 64.

This is the oldest surviving signed and dated shawl design in any Paris collection.

Detail of long shawl. France, c. 1820. Woven *au lancé*, trimmed on back side, silk and wool; the fringes are sewn on separately, 300 × 139 cm/118 × 54½ in. Paris, author's collection, no. 12.
Exhibited: Paris, 1982, cat. no. 37.

The pine corner ornament has undergone a transformation into a small bunch of flowers tied with a ribbon: only the arrangement of the decoration makes it possible to classify this shawl as a "cashmere" type. At the request of certain Paris manufacturers, the designers temporarily avoided the imitation of the Oriental patterns.

On pages 66–67: long shawl with border of harlequin pines (detail). France, c. 1820–25. Woven *au lancé*, trimmed on back, silk and cotton; the borders were woven separately and the harlequin fringing sewn on separately; 320 × 135 cm/ 126 × 53 in. Paris, author's collection, no. 2.

Four large pines alternate with three and two waisted semi-pines.

Lop-sided shawl (*châle boiteux*), known as such because it has only one border, with eight pines. France, 1820–30. Woven *au lancé*, trimmed on back, silk and wool; fringing sewn on to the single border; 136 × 139 cm/53½ × 54¾ in. Paris, author's collection, no. 7. Exhibited: Paris, 1982, cat. no. 41.

Opposite: long shawl with border consisting of eight pines (detail). France, 1820–30. Woven *au lancé*, trimmed on back, silk and wool; the fringes have been sewn on separately; 292 × 141 cm/ 115 × 55½ in. Paris, author's collection, no. 9.

Long shawl, border decoration of eight pines (detail).
France, 1820–30.
Woven *au lancé*, trimmed on back, silk and wool; fringes sewn on separately; 304 × 138 cm/ 119¾ × 54¼ in.
Paris, author's collection, no. 43.

The curling vertices of the pines end in split layers, with three roots at their bases. Their shape is outlined by a border of clear ground.

Opposite: detail of long shawl with border consisting of nine harlequin pine compartments.
Woven *au lancé*, trimmed on back, wool and silk, 312 × 155 cm/123 × 61 in.
Paris, author's collection, no. 47.

The harlequin ground colour of each smaller pine compartment of the gallery contrasts with the ground colour of the pine compartment below it. In order to obtain particularly brilliant colours, the warp threads were dyed before weaving.

Below left: square shawl with medallions.
France, 1815–20.
Woven *au lancé*, trimmed on back; silk, cotton and wool, 134 × 136 cm/52¾ × 53½ in.
Paris, author's collection, no. 6
Exhibited: Paris, 1982, cat. no. 52

Below right: square shawl with medallions.
France, 1820–30.
Woven *au lancé*, trimmed on back; silk, cotton and wool, 152 × 152 cm/60 × 60 in.
Paris, author's collection, no. 16.

Opposite: detail of a square turn-over shawl folded into a triangle, the border decoration consisting of 20 pines.
Woven in Kashmir, c. 1810, subsequently finished in France.
Twill-tapestry weave, cashmere, 164 × 162 cm/

64½ × 63¾ in.
Paris, Au Fils du Temps.

The border of the less ornate corner was sewn on in reverse so that when this corner was folded over, both decorated sections were displayed, one above the other.

These two shawls with small medallions have a fittingly restrained design and colouring as they would have been worn with more simply-cut, informal clothes. Square shawls enjoyed considerable popularity after 1830 and manufacturers produced proportionately fewer long shawls.

On pages 74–75: striped square shawl with medallion decoration in the corners (detail).
France, 1825–35.
Woven *au lancé*, trimmed on back, cashmere (?), 180 × 180 cm/71 × 71 in.
Paris, author's collection, no. 17.
Exhibited: Paris, 1982, cat. no. 48.

A quarter medallion is superimposed in each corner, on a field of stripes with branch motif, giving an impression of transparency and depth.

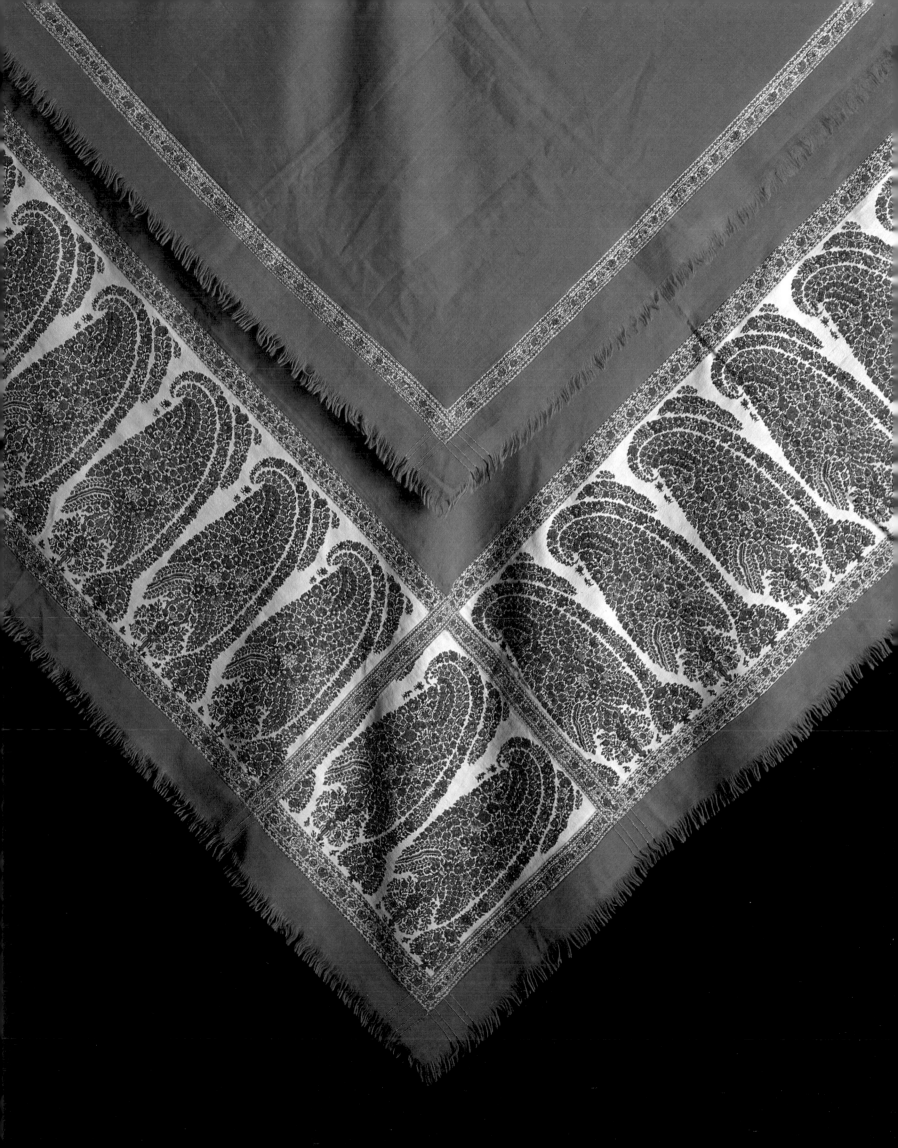

On pages 76–77: striped scarf (detail).
Northwest India, first half of the nineteenth century Woven in twill tapestry in three separate long pieces, cashmere, 268 × 61.5 cm/ 105½ × 24¼ in.
Paris, author's collection, no. 66

This type of striped weave, with no borders, is called a *jamewar* or gown piece in its native country.

Below: design for a shawl, called *Isfahan*, signed Amédée Couder.
Paris Exhibition, 1834.
Gouache on paper, 33.5 × 32.5 cm/13¼ × 12¾ in.
Paris, Musée National des Techniques, C.N.A.M. no. 10.334.
Exhibited: Paris, 1982, cat. no. 85b; Lyons, 1983, cat. no. 65.
This is the first known "quartered shawl."
The Arabic inscriptions, enclosed in cartouches, give the date and place of the National Exhibition as well as the names of the shawl's creators: the designer, Couder, and the manufacturer, Gaussen. A shawl of this design was sold at auction in Paris in December 1981. Its purchaser was kind enough to allow it to be exhibited in Paris in 1982, cat. no. 82, and in Lyons in 1983, cat. no. 23.
A detail of the design is shown on the opposite page.

Right: plates nos. 10 and 11 from the album *Souvenir de l'Exposition des Produits de l'Industrie Française de 1839* showing Hérault & Léon's shawl design which was subsequently woven by the Paris manufacturer Bournhonet, Ternaux's successor.
Paris, Bibliothèque Forney.

Opposite: long shawl with pseudo-Gothic decoration (detail).
Woven in Paris in 1839 by Bournhonet, to the design shown on this page.
Woven *au lancé*, trimmed on back, cashmere, 309 × 169 cm/121½ × 66½ in.
London, Victoria and Albert Museum, no. T. 362–1980.

This is one of the so-called "Renaissance" shawls which were introduced from 1834. Below the ornamental motif of the cathedral there are four giant pines; flowers radiating from their apices look like exploding fireworks.

Last plate in the album *Souvenir de l'Exposition des Produits de l'Industrie Française de 1839*, reproducing a shawl design by Amédée Couder, which was woven by the Paris manufacturer, Gaussen. Paris, Bibliothèque Forney.

Advances in weaving on the Jacquard loom had made it possible to weave shawls which repeated the design only once lengthwise and once across the width. This meant that a design, which could be up to 90 cm/35½ in wide, was reproduced four times in one shawl. The left-hand half had to be identical to the right-hand half, whether a mirror image or not. This engraving is interesting in that it shows the artist's breadth of inspiration, which the weaver could never hope to reproduce exactly. This shawl was called the *Nou-Rouz*, after the Persian New Year or Festival of Flowers. A procession of dignitaries is depicted, mounted on horses, camels and elephants, on their way to pay their solemn respects to their monarch, the Shah. Under the ogival arches which ornament the shawl's border, a lively celebration involving musicians and dancers is taking place, with exotic birds fluttering overhead.

Opposite: long shawl, known as the *Nou-Rouz* (detail). Paris, 1839, woven by Gaussen, after Amédée Couder's design shown on this page. Woven *au lancé*, trimmed on back, cashmere, 389 × 165 cm/153 × 65 in. Milan, Etro collection, no. 50.
Exhibited: Lyons, 1983, cat. no. 26.

The extremely complicated decorative scheme of this shawl involved the use of more than 100,000 punched cards. Twelve colours were used for the weft.
The Victoria and Albert Museum, London, houses another shawl of this design, which was exhibited in Paris in 1982, cat. no. 84.

Opposite: detail of the central section of the *Nou-Rouz* shawl shown on page 83.

Below: lower center section detail of the main border of the shawl shown on page 83.

On page 86: detail of the upper center section of the main border of the shawl shown on page 83.

On page 87: a corner of the "procession" which forms the gallery in the shawl shown on page 83. The Islamic-inspired stylized scrollwork between the columns is purely to add further embellishment to the profusion of ornamentation.

Design for the *Nou-Rouz* shawl, signed by Amédée Couder, National Exhibition, Paris, 1839. Gouache on paper, 77.5 × 32.5 cm/30½ × 12¾ in. Paris, Musée National des Techniques, C.N.A.M., no. 10.333.
Exhibited: Paris, 1982, cat. no. 85c; Lyons, 1983, cat. no. 66.

As seen in the engraving of this design, the artist gave free rein to his imagination; note the differences between the two central motifs.

Opposite: detail of the plate from the album *Souvenir de l'Exposition des Produits de l'Industrie Française de 1839*, reproduced on page 82.

89

Square shawl with
medallion.
France, c. 1840.
Woven *au lancé*, trimmed
on back, cashmere, 198 ×
186 cm/78 × 73 in.
Paris, Aux Fils du Temps.

Twenty-four small pines
are scattered over the
black field between the
central medallion and the
corner quarter medallions.
The medallion
circumference is decorated
with Gothic-style details.
Both the horizontal borders
have the word PHENIX
(phoenix) woven into them,
twice right way round and
twice in mirror image.
During the period 1840–50
some of the most famous
Paris manufacturers gave
their shawls names. This
example originally had
shawl ends in blocks of
different colours. The
harlequin shawl ends seen
here, which are hand
embroidered, must have
been sewn on in place of
the original ends, between
1855 and 1860, to bring the
shawl up to date with the
prevailing fashion.

Opposite: detail of the
square shawl shown on
this page; this blow-up of
the border has been
displayed perpendicularly
to the usual way.
Therefore, the word
PHENIX has to be read
vertically.

Long shawl, main border decorated with six pines (detail).
Northwest India, c. 1840–45.
Twill-tapestry, cashmere, woven in several rectangular pieces, 328 × 142 cm/129 × 56 in. Milan, Etro collection, no. 23.

The surrounds of the three pairs of pines facing each other which form the border have a transparent effect since they are defined only by a white outline. Lotus flowers spread out in a fan shape between the confronted pines. Medallions, also decorated with lotus

flowers, link the pines which are back to back. All these motifs are repeated in the gallery. This shawl can be linked in type with the shawl shown in plate no. 16 of the Yale catalogue, 1975.

Detail of long shawl with pine-decorated border. Europe, c. 1840. Woven *au lancé*, trimmed on back, wool, 337 × 161 cm/132¾ × 63½ in. Milan, Etro collection, no. 60

The motif is contained in a rectangle and is repeated four times on each border. It is composed of three pines of varying size; the smallest has its apex pointing downwards. A sword of some type separates the compartments containing the motifs.

Long shawl with a border comprising six pines (detail).
France, c. 1840.
Woven *au lancé*, trimmed on back cashmere (?), 363 × 161 cm/143 × 63½ in.
Milan, Etro collection, no. 59.

From about 1835–40 pines were often arranged in pairs, adorsed or confronted, and were fewer in number. The single colour field has grown smaller and the corner ornaments open out like fans.

Λ sumptuous shawl with rich tones – the weft comprises nine colours – its ornamentation is further enhanced by the fan motifs which decorate the corners of the central field. The decoration can be compared with the cashmere shawl on page 42, made in Paris by Chambellan & Duché.

Opposite: detail of the shawl shown above.

on back, wool 188 ×
188 cm/74 × 74 in.
Paris, author's collection,
no. 24.
Exhibited: Paris, 1982, cat.
no. 106.

acanthus leaves. By this
time square shawls were
larger; the decoration
covered all the material and
their rich colours meant
that they could be worn
with the most elegant
clothes.

Square shawl.
France, 1840–45.
Woven *au lancé*, trimmed
on back, cashmere (?),
180 × 180 cm/71 × 71 in.
Paris, author's collection,
no. 45.
Exhibited: Lyons, 1983,
not included in exhibition
catalogue.

This shawl, in the
"Renaissance" style, has
motifs enclosed in broken
arches.

Signed and dated design
for a shawl *à pivot* by
Berrus, 1849
Gouache on paper, 66.4 ×
30.2 cm/26 × 12 in.
Paris, Musée des Arts
Décoratifs, Cabinet des
Dessins, no. CD5436.3.
Exhibited: Lyons, 1983,
cat. no. 67.

This shawl is decorated
exclusively by plant forms
with bold stylization which
was well in advance of its
time. The horizontal
borders have vanished.
Some plants have
encroached on the vertical
borders.

Design for a quarter of a shawl.
Folio no. 1 of Berrus's album covering XX48/2, 1848/50.
Gouache on paper, 48.4 × 23 cm/19 × 9 in.
Paris, Musée des Arts Décoratifs, Cabinet des Dessins, no. CD5275, F.1.

This design by Berrus can be compared with the shawl shown in plate no.

50 of John Irwin's book *Shawls* (1955). With the exception of the horizontal border and the harlequin shawl ends, they are identical.
The purely imaginary vegetation, luxuriant and fantastic, paints a picture of an exotic landscape. The vertical and horizontal borders differ in ornamentation and in width.

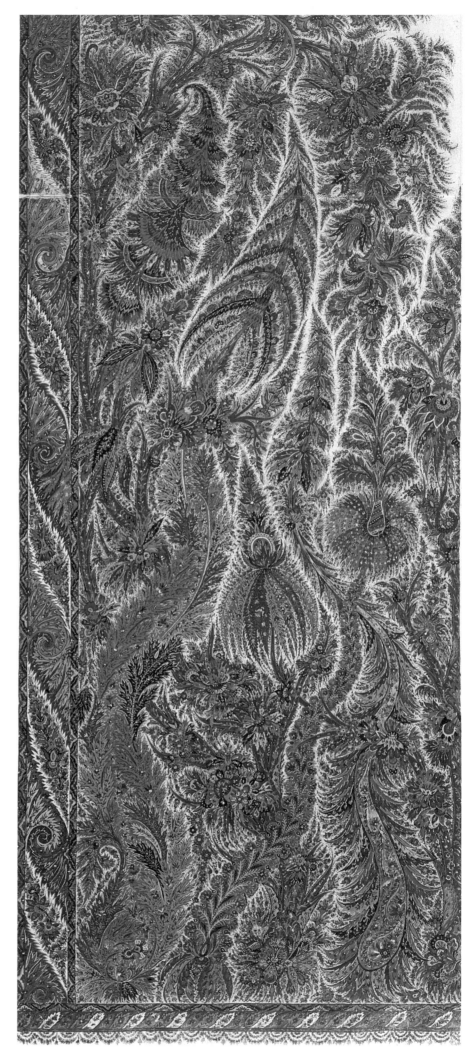

Design for a shawl.
Folio no. 2 from Berrus's album, XX48/2, dated 1848/50.
Gouache on paper, 38.5 × 23 cm/15¼ × 9 in.
Paris, Musée des Arts Décoratifs, Cabinet des Dessins, no. CD5275, F.2.

This exuberant design has made use of plants as well as classic pine motifs of varying sizes around the central decoration. The large pines break into the horizontal borders. The two halves of the central section are mirror images of one another along a vertical axis, while the large pines at each end are also repeated along the same axis but not as a mirror image.

Detail of Berrus's stamp as it appears on this design.

Design for a shawl. Folio no. 3 of Berrus's album, XX48/2, dated 1848–50. Gouache on paper, 38.5 × 23 cm/15¼ × 9 in. Paris, Musée des Arts Décoratifs, Cabinet des Dessins, no. CD5275, F.3.

This shawl owes its effect to a double contrast. The border motifs stand out against a white ground, while in the center section the floral ornamentation forms the background on which the white ground seems to form a tracery. This center section is symmetrical in relation to the two axes, while the large pine motif is repeated, but not as a mirror image, along the vertical axis.

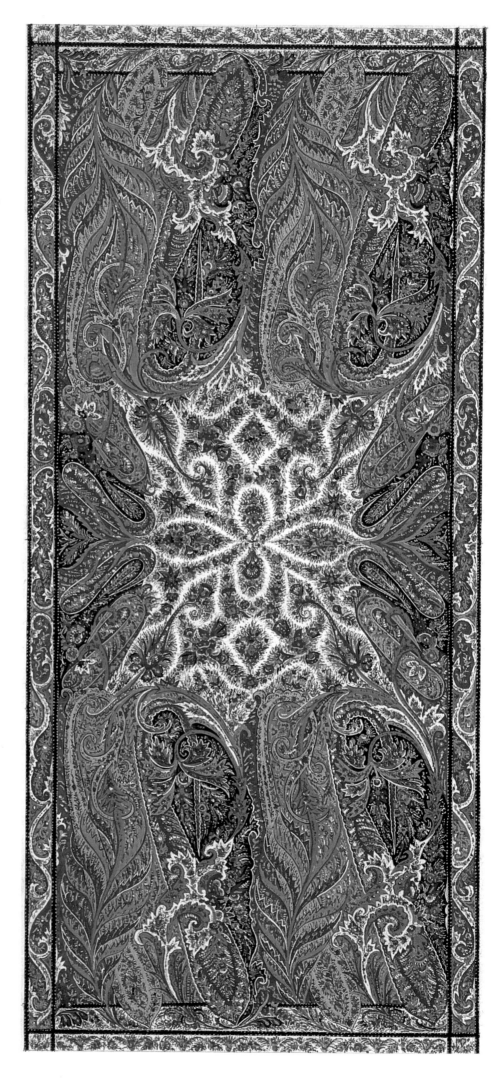

Design for a shawl by
Berrus. Folio no. 4 from his
album XX48/2, dated
1848–50.
Gouache on paper, 38.5 ×
23 cm/15¼ × 9 in.
Paris, Musée des Arts
Décoratifs, Cabinet des
Dessins, no. CD5275, F.4.

Here the pattern is
repeated as a whole in
mirror image along the
vertical and horizontal
axes. The flowering
branches which stretch
towards the center form a
modified X. The horizontal
and vertical borders have
almost disappeared,
replaced by a black ribbon
which meanders along the
edge as a framework for
the decoration.

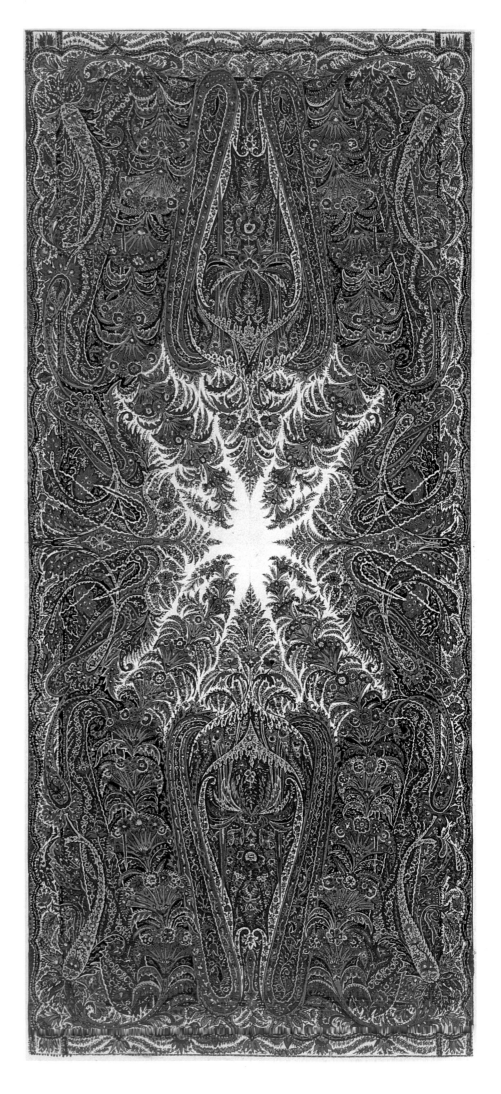

Design for a quarter of a shawl.
Folio no. 5 from Berrus's album XX48/2, dated 1848–50.
Gouache on paper, 38.5 × 23 cm/15¼ × 9 in.
Paris, Musée des Arts Décoratifs, Cabinet des Dessins, no. CD5275, F.5.

Berrus has organized his design so that the decorative motif is repeated symmetrically along the two axes. When completed the shawl would show a tree of life, standing out in a relief of white ground against the sinuous, intertwining shapes that herald the palm tree trunks which appear in the shawl shown on page 114.

Design for a shawl. Folio no. 6 from Berrus's album XX48/2, dated 1848–50. Gouache on paper, 38.5 × 23 cm/15¼ × 9 in. Paris, Musée des Arts Décoratifs, Cabinet des Dessins, no. CD5275, F.6.

The designs in Berrus's album (the first six of which are reproduced on these pages) illustrate his ''*style végétal*:'' luxuriant arrangements of plant life, either singly or combined with the pine motif. This album was shown at the Paris exhibition of shawls held in 1982, cat. no. 128. The decoration here is symmetrical in relation to the vertical axis. Only the area between the central field and the borders is reflected as a mirror image along the horizontal axis. A lush meander of leaves garlands the edge of the shawl and takes the place of both vertical and horizontal borders.

Design for a shawl *à pivot*, signed and dated by Berrus, 1848, Paris Exhibition, 1849. Gouache on paper, 33 × 15.3 cm/13 × 6 in. Paris, Musée des Arts Décoratifs, Cabinet des Dessins, no. CD5319.

The very wide vertical borders inside the outer frame repeat symmetrically about the two axes. In the middle section of the shawl design the scheme is arranged differently: the pattern is repeated only once, pivoting around a central point. Hence the term *"à pivot."* As the decoration of the middle section is repeated only once instead of three times (as in "quartered" shawls), a great deal more work was involved in the preparation of the point-papers. Predictably, therefore, this type of shawl is rare.

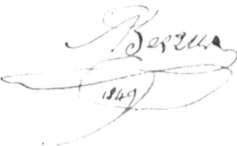

Detail of Berrus's signature as shown on the design on page 106.

Design for a shawl signed and dated by Berrus, 1849. Paris Exhibition, 1849. Gouache on paper, 32.2 × 17.3 cm/ 12¾ × 6¾ in. Paris, Musée des Arts Décoratifs, Cabinet des Dessins, no. CD5320.

The ornamentation on this shawl is symmetrical in relation to the vertical axis. Only the main areas of decoration on either end are in mirror image about the horizontal axis. The borders have been eliminated and the pines are mixed in with the vegetation.

Design for a shawl *à pivot*, signed and dated by Berrus, 1849; exhibited at the Paris Exhibition, 1849. Gouache on paper, 32.6 × 15.6 cm/12¾ × 6¼ in. Paris, Musée des Arts Décoratifs, Cabinet des Dessins, no. CD5323.

The entire ornamentation of this shawl pivots around the center point (with the exception of the vertical borders that are symmetrical in relation to the vertical and horizontal axis), giving a diagonal effect which is shown to be particularly effective in this design.

Another Berrus shawl design, signed and dated (1849); exhibited at the Paris Exhibition of that same year.
Gouache on paper, 35.2 × 17 cm/13¾ × 6¾ in.
Paris, Musée des Arts Décoratifs, Cabinet des Dessins, no. CD5321.

The slim and sinuous pines surround a tree of life which is set against four differently coloured fields. The tree has only vertical symmetry while the remainder of the decoration is mirror-imaged in relation to both axes. The varying background colours give the impression of a great diversity of ornamentation; on close examination the motifs on these fields are revealed as identical.

Signed and dated design for a double *à pivot* shawl by Berrus, 1849; Paris Exhibition, 1849. Gouache on paper, 49.2 × 24.3 cm/19½ × 9½ in. Paris, Musée des Arts Décoratifs, Cabinet des Dessins, no. CD5322.

The left-hand and the right-hand side are *à pivot* designs and give a mirror image of each other. In the center section the decorative motifs stand out against fields of three contrasting colours. As we have seen in the Berrus designs shown on previous pages, the fringed shawl ends have festoon motifs. But here, by contrast, these motifs appear against harlequin backgrounds, prompting the thought that this shawl may signal a turning point in Berrus's designs, when he abandoned his former avoidance of harlequin shawl ends and succumbed to the prevailing fashion. His shawl designs subsequently all had polichrome fringes.

Opposite: square shawl. Paris, manufactured by Frédéric Hébert & Son, c. 1852.
Woven *au lancé* trimmed on back, cashmere, 190 × 188 cm/ 74¾ × 74 in.
Paris, author's collection, no. 39.
Exhibited: Paris, 1982, cat. no. 175; Lyons, 1983, cat. no. 55.

Eight pairs of small pines surround the cruciform central field. Four stand out against differently coloured backgrounds. The wearer, by folding, could choose from four colour schemes.

Detail of the inscription woven in white in the left-hand corner of the field of the shawl shown on the opposite page. A certain amount of comparison with other similar shawls was necessary to decipher: ''H. Cachemire pur.'' (H stood for the manufacturer, Hébert.)

Records in the Prudhommes registry, Paris, confirm that this inscription was registered as a trade mark on 25th August, 1852. It does not seem too fanciful to make out a phoenix, albeit extremely stylized, at the tip of the corner ornament, with long curling tail feathers.

Opposite: long shawl, border decorated with five pines (detail). Northwest India, c. 1845–50. Twill-tapestry, cashmere, woven in several rectangular pieces, 334 × 141 cm/131½ × 55½ in. Paris, Aux Fils du Temps.

The pines, 90 cm/35½ in high, give the impression of pushing the inner horizontal border, towards the center section, thereby forming five arches.

Detail of long shawl with a border decorated with three groups of pines. Northwest India, c. 1845–50. Twill-tapestry, cashmere, woven in several rectangular pieces, 310 × 142 cm/122 × 55⅞ in. Paris, author's collection, no. 73.

Here the pines have grown over the inner horizontal border, traces of which are discernible in the background.

Opposite: detail of long
shawl with deep border,
typical of the "*style
végétal.*"
Paris, c. 1850.
Woven *au lancé*, trimmed
on back, cashmere, 383 ×
166 cm/150¾ × 63 in.
Paris, author's collection,
no. 26.
Exhibited: Paris, 1982, cat.
no. 113; Lyons, 1983, cat.
no. 39.

The decorative scheme of
this shawl is reminiscent of
Berrus's designs during
the years 1848–50, and of
the example on page 103
in particular. The
composition is similar.
Here two palm trees
intertwine on both sides of
the tree of life. The
inclusion of animals make
it a rarity, as does its
exceptionally rich range of
colours: the weft is made
up of no fewer than 12
colours.

Detail of the shawl on page
114, showing a snake.

Detail of the shawl
illustrated on page 114,
showing a butterfly.

Opposite: detail of the
shawl on page 114,
showing a salamander.

Note the exceptionally fine
weaving which results in
precise and supple
delineation of the motifs.

Opposite: detail of a long shawl: *à pivot* design. Paris, c. 1850.
Woven *au lancé*, trimmed on back, cashmere, 360 × 158 cm/141¾ × 62¼ in. Paris, author's collection, no. 40.
Exhibited: Paris, 1982, cat. no. 114; Lyons, 1983, cat. no. 43.

An astounding technical achievement, given the width of the decorative scheme; there are nine colours in the weft. This shawl's design is a good example of an artistic compromise between the traditional cashmere style, incorporating pines and making a feature of their curled apices, and the "*style végétal.*" The pines are graduated in size and accentuate the diagonal, off-center effect of an *à pivot* design.

Detail of the center section of the shawl *à pivot* shown on the opposite page.

Design for a shawl signed
by Berrus. Great Exhibition,
London, 1851.
Gouache on paper, 79 ×
30.5 cm/31 × 12 in.
Paris, Musée National des
Techniques, C.N.A.M., no.
8.797.

The same motif is repeated
in parallel on either side of
the vertical axis, the only
repeat in the center of the
shawl; the two main areas
of decoration are mirror
images along the horizontal
axis.

Opposite, left: design for a
shawl, signed by Berrus,
Great Exhibition, London,
1851.
Gouache on paper, 73 × 35
cm/28¾ × 13¾ in.
Paris, Musée National des
Techniques, C.N.A.M., no.
8.797.

The design is symmetrical
in relation to the vertical
axis, and the *pentes* are
mirror images along the
horizontal axis. Note the
four differently coloured
backgrounds in the center.

Opposite, right: design for
a shawl, signed by Berrus.
Great Exhibition, London,
1851.
Gouache on paper, 75 × 35
cm/29½ × 13¾ in.
Paris, Musée National des
Techniques, C.N.A.M., no.
8.797.

The organization of the
design is identical to that
reproduced on the left. In
place of the pines,
architectural motifs make a
discreet appearance
among the luxuriant plant
life. The three shawl
designs shown on these
pages were exhibited
together in the same frame
in Paris in 1982, cat. no.
129.

123

Square shawl, Europe, c. 1850
Woven *au lancé*, trimmed on back, wool, 187 × 180 cm/73½ × 70¾ in. Milan, Etro collection, no. 25.

The decoration of leaves and flowers, the festoon which forms a border all round the edge of the shawl and the four different colours of the central field were all typical of "four seasons shawls." The owner of such a shawl would have folded it carefully before draping it around her shoulders so as to display the colour which best harmonized with the clothes she was wearing.

Opposite: center section of the shawl shown below. The floral decoration echoes Berrus's design during the years 1848–50 but does not necessarily suggest that the shawl was woven in France, since Berrus sold his designs throughout Europe.

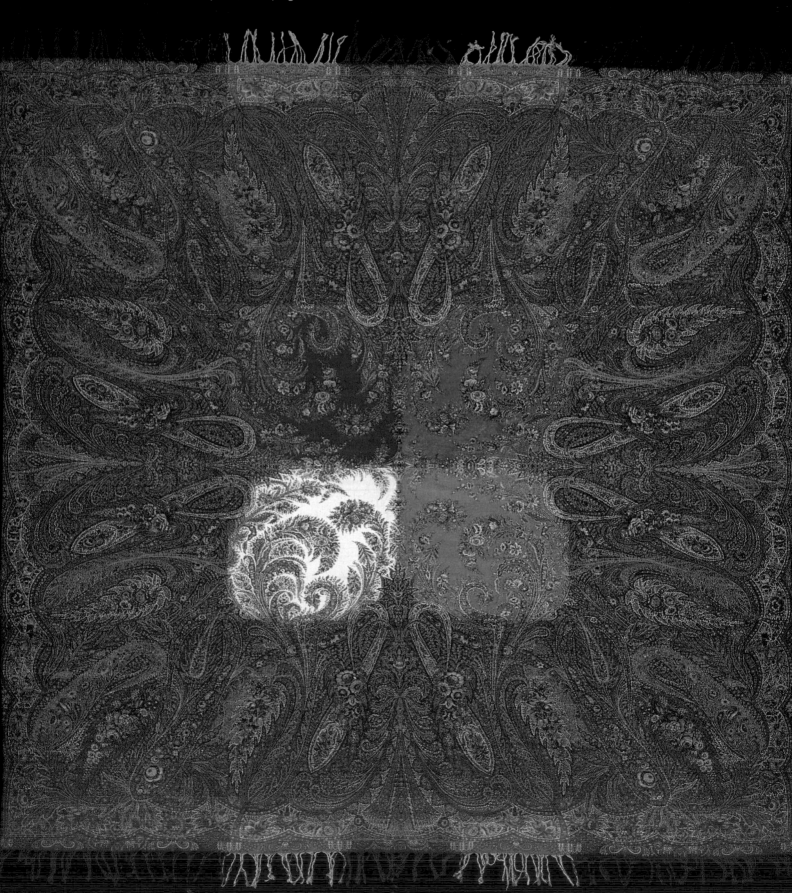

Signed shawl design by Berrus. Universal Exhibition, Paris, 1855. Gouache on paper, 87.5 × 32.5 cm/34½ × 12¾ in. Paris, Musée National des Techniques, C.N.A.M., no. 8.800.1.

There is a strong architectural feel to this design. Pines are set in *mihrabs* (niches in the walls inside mosques to show the direction of Mecca), endowing them with the status of sacred objects.

Long shawl (lower half). Paris, 1855. Woven *au lancé*, trimmed on back, cashmere, 353 × 154 cm/139 × 60½ in. Paris, author's collection, no. 42.

With the exception of the central pine and its niche, all the motifs which appear in Berrus's design on this page are woven into the shawl. The Arms of England are woven into the corners. It is probable that this shawl was commissioned from a Paris manufacturer by a member of the Royal Family. The texture of the weave is exceptionally fine, as are the threads used, which in part explains the piece's poor state of repair.

On page 128: central section of the shawl shown on page 127.

On page 129: detail of side portion of the shawl shown on page 127.

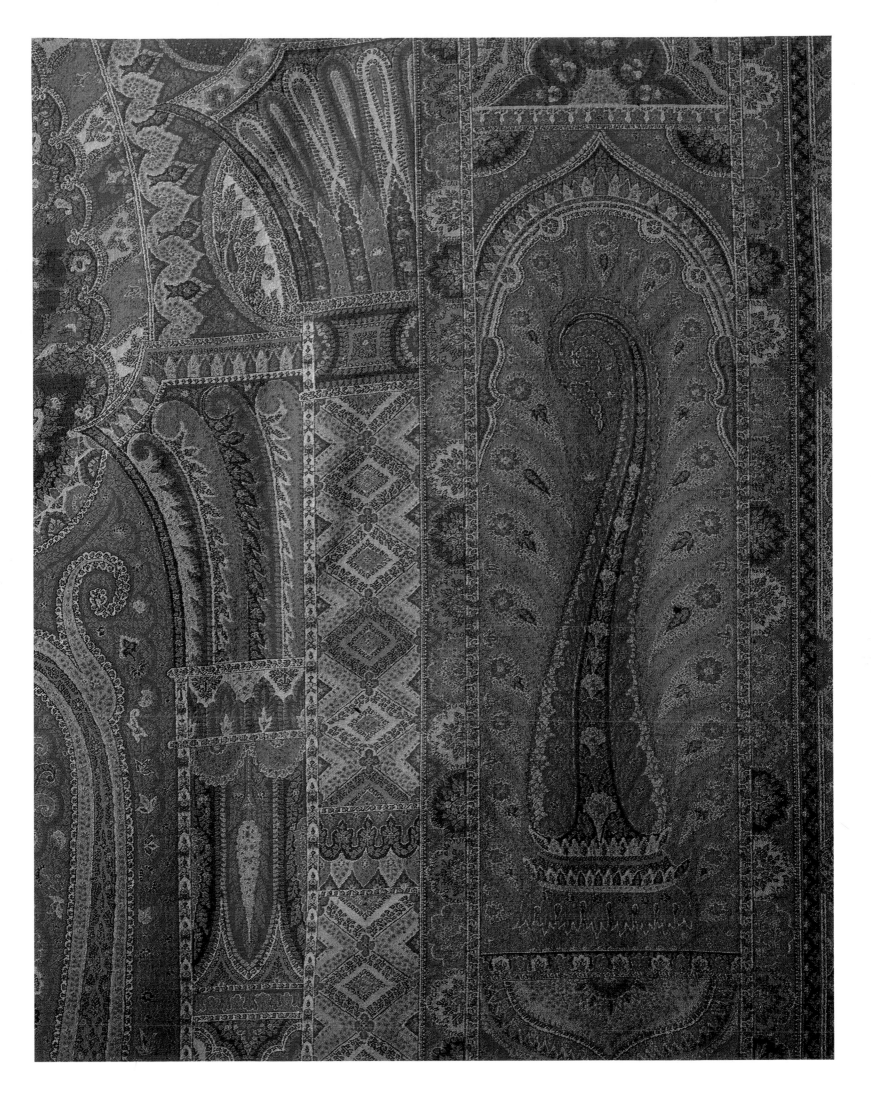

Border and harlequin shawl end of the shawl on page 127.

In the right-hand corner the royal Arms of England, reversed (see page 184); the designs are always rendered the right way round in the lower left corner and the upper right corner when the shawl has a mirror-image design in relation to the two symmetrical axes.

Opposite, left: shawl
design, signed by Berrus.
Paris Exhibition, 1855.
Gouache on paper, 44 ×
20.5 cm/17¼ × 8⅛ in.
Paris, Musée National des
Techniques, C.N.A.M., no.
8.800.1.

Decoration reminiscent of
carved wall panelling and
rococo bronzes.

Opposite, right: signed
shawl design by Berrus.
Paris Exhibition, 1855.
Gouache on paper, 43.5 ×
21 cm/17 × 8¼ in.
Paris, Musée National des
Techniques, C.N.A.M., no.
8.800.2.

Over the basic rococo
design are superimposed
particularly highly stylized
pines combined with plant
motifs. In the center, a
niche encloses a central
pine with what appears to
be a number of pendants
suspended from it.

Signed shawl design by
Berrus, Paris Exhibition,
1855.
Gouache on paper, 44 ×
20.5 cm/17¼ × 8 in.
Paris, Musée National des
Techniques, C.N.A.M., no.
8.800.1.

An intriguing synthesis has
been achieved between
floral and architectural
motifs in this shawl. On
either side of an altar-like
construction, are three
graduated arches; resting
on their columns are slim
pedestals and a balustrade.
Each arch contains a pine
or a flowering branch. A
vase of flowers is centrally
placed below some
drapery, and similar
ornaments occupy the top
of the balustrade. Similar
motifs are used on a
smaller scale for the more
intricate ornamentation
below.

Shawl design signed by Berrus. Paris Exhibition, 1855.
Gouache on paper, 43.5 × 21 cm/17 × 8¼ in.
Paris, Musée National des Techniques, C.N.A.M., no. 8.800.2.

In this synthesis of Persian- and Chinese-inspired motifs, a panel in the form of a *mihrab* contains the outline of a Turkish or Chinese pavilion; behind it a cedar is flanked by trees in blossom. On either side are two pagodas: their tip-tilted eaves, although reminiscent of China, are topped by Islamic-style crescent moons. Some steps, depicted in the Chinese style with a vertical perspective, lead through Persian gardens. On either side of the center panel, pagodas are shown atop one another in the side panel.

Shawl design signed by Berrus. Paris Exhibition, 1855.
Gouache on paper, 43.5 × 20.5 cm/17 × 8 in.
Paris, Musée National des Techniques, C.N.A.M., no. 8.800.2.

As in the example reproduced on the opposite page, this design incorporates a *mihrab*-shaped panel and it contains a strange building, part Chinese, part Islamic in style. The entire ornamentation of the shawl is symmetrical in relation to the vertical axis; only the *pentes* are in mirror image.

Design for a shawl *à pivot*, signed by Berrus. Paris Exhibition, 1855.
Gouache on paper, 87 × 33 cm/34¼ × 13 in.
Paris, Musée National des Techniques, C.N.A.M., no. 8.800.2.

This *à pivot* design has resulted in the large central motif being diagonal and the sweeps of drapery complement the fantastical and baroque architectural features of the end sections.

An *à pivot* shawl design, signed by Berrus. Paris Exhibition, 1855. Gouache on paper, 43.5 × 20.5 cm/17 × 8 in. Paris, Musée National des Techniques, C.N.A.M., no. 8.800.2.

Four pines confronted in pairs, with bases scrolling in spreads in the corners of the shawl, are flanked by groups of smaller sloping pines. In the center the decoration consists of a delicate floral motif. To a certain extent the elaborate composition obscures the diagonal effect typical of *à pivot* shawl designs. Although very different in style, there are some features that are reminiscent of the shawl shown on page 120. The French Imperial Arms are drawn on the harlequin shawl ends, suggesting perhaps that this shawl was commissioned by the Empress Eugénie. The five preceding shawl designs were grouped together within the same frame when they were shown at the 1982 Paris Exhibition, cat. no. 129.

Long shawl (detail).
France, 1855.
Woven *au lancé*, trimmed
on back, wool, 350 ×
159 cm/137¾ × 62½ in.
Milan, Etro collection, no.
58.

In the left-hand corner the
inscription ''Paris
Exposition 1855'' can be
made out. The quarter
medallions in the corners
are rare in long shawls.

Long shawl (detail).
Paris, c. 1855.
Woven *au lancé*, trimmed
on back, wool, 363 ×
163 cm/143 × 64¼ in.
Milan, Etro collection.

The initials F. M. have been
woven into the two left-
hand corners, indicating
that the shawl was
manufactured by the Paris
house of Fortier & Maillard,
considered to be "the
most outstanding
producers of striped
shawls."

Long shawl (detail). Europe, c. 1850–55. Woven *au lancé*, trimmed on back, wool, 340 × 160 cm/133¾ × 63 in. Milan, Etro collection, no. 27.

The plant decoration in this shawl consists of the same design woven in parallel: the contrast is provided by the use of differently coloured warp threads for the two central fields. The white ground on the left throws the red weft threads surrounding it into brilliant relief. The contrast between the green warp threads used for the right-hand field and the surrounding reds is less sharply defined since the two tones are closer in the spectrum. This example shows the importance of dyeing the warp threads, at a time when it was not feasible to reproduce the intricacies of the design motifs faithfully.

Opposite: detail of the center of the deep border (*pentes*) in the shawl shown above.

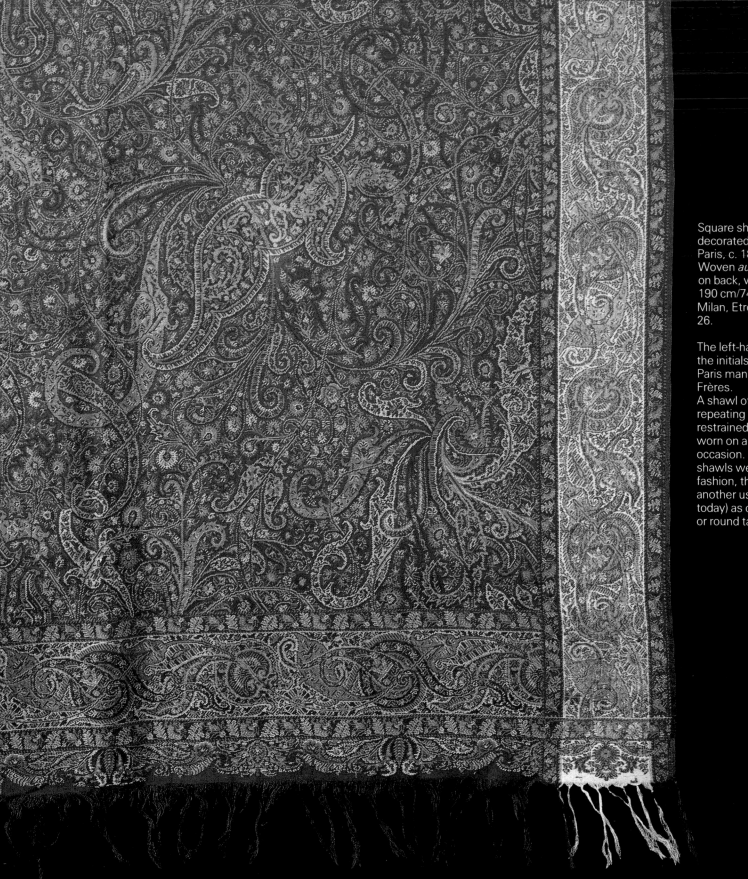

Square shawl with all-over decorated ground (detail). Paris, c. 1850–55. Woven *au lancé*, trimmed on back, wool, 190 × 190 cm/74¾ × 74¾ in. Milan, Etro collection, no. 26.

The left-hand corner bears the initials L.F., for the Paris manufacturers Lion Frères.
A shawl of this type, with a repeating design and restrained effect could be worn on almost any occasion. When cashmere shawls went out of fashion, they found another use (and still do today) as covers for square or round tables.

Long shawl decorated with
four groups of three pines
(detail).
Paris, c. 1855–60.
Woven *au lancé*, trimmed
on back, cashmere, 347 ×
166 cm/136½ × 65¼ in.
Paris, author's collection,
no. 46.
Exhibited: Lyons, 1983,
cat. no. 42.

In the left-hand corners, the
Parisian manufacturers,
Lion Frères, have woven
their initials, L.F. The
border comprises four tall
rectangles; each of these
compartments contains
three pines, with a
climbing plant twisted
round them. The inner
horizontal border has been
omitted (see shawl on
page 112).

Design for a quarter of a long shawl with Antony Berrus's stamp, not signed, c. 1855–60. Gouache on gelatin, 41.8 × 32 cm/16½ × 12½ in.
Paris, Musée des Arts Décoratifs, Cabinet des Dessins, no. CD5436,13.

The geometrically inspired decorative composition runs along parallel lines. Berrus has conjured up a design reminiscent of a mosaic or similar architectural embellishment.

Design for a quarter of a long shawl. Stamped Antony Berrus, not signed, c. 1855–60.
Gouache on gelatin, 45.4 × 24 cm/17¾ × 9½ in.
Paris, Musée des Arts Décoratifs, Cabinet des Dessins, no. CD5436,16.

This design repeats many of the decorative motifs used for the shawl shown on page 137, with the curled pines and the pendant smaller pines.

Design for a quarter of a long shawl. Stamped Antony Berrus, not signed, c. 1855–60.
Gouache on gelatin, 48 × 32 cm/19 × 12½ in. Paris, Musée des Arts Décoratifs, Cabinet des Dessins, no. CD5436,17.

The floral composition of this design contrasts strongly with the design on page 144. The vase of flowers in the center of the motif is also present in the design on page 144, but there it is a small and inconspicuous detail. In this example there is an interesting derivant of the pine motif, made up of what appears to be overlapping butterfly wings. A very wide border surrounds the decoration, rounded at the corners.

Shawl design signed by Berrus. Great Exhibition, London, 1862.
Pencil and wash on paper, 95 × 39.3 cm/37½ × 15½ in.
Paris, Musée des Arts Décoratifs, Cabinet des Dessins, no. CD5436,20.

The crowned female figure seated on a throne may represent Queen Victoria, which suggests this design could be a tribute to the country that hosted the Great Exhibition. The patterns shown on the layers of drapery hanging from the throne give a retrospective view of the various styles of cashmere shawls: first comes an example of the border decorated with small pines, then the use of large pines and finally, in the background, the "*style végétal*," decorated with plant life. On either side of the central scene, panels with intricate ornamentation are like columns supporting a sculptured pediment.

Design for a *burnous*
shawl. Gonelle Frères,
1861.
The inscription states:
"cashmere style.
registered patent,
manufactured by Robert &
Gosselin, 1862."
Gouache on paper, 54.3 ×
28.8 cm/21⅜ × 11⅜ in.
Paris, Musée des Arts
Décoratifs, Cabinet des
Dessins, no. CD5304,11.
Exhibited: Paris, 1982, cat.
no. 138; Lyons, 1983, cat.
no. 69

In January 1987 a shawl of
this design was acquired at
a public auction sale in
Paris by the Musée de la
Mode et du Costume de la
Ville de Paris. It is now
numbered 87.2.2. in the
museum's collection, and
measures 315 × 138.5 cm/
10 ft 3 in × 4 ft 5 in.
We believe it is the only
burnous shawl actually
known.
The characteristic of the
burnous shawl is that its
central field, being halfway
between the two end
borders, is closer to one
side border than to the
other. Its decoration, like
that of the *à pivot* shawls,
is only repeated once in the
length of the shawl.

Three photographs taken in 1862, each showing Gonelle's shawl (shown on the opposite page) worn in a different way.

The photographs measure 17.4 × 11.5 cm/6⅞ × 4½ in.
Paris, Musée des Arts Décoratifs, Cabinet des Dessins, no. DOC12. Exhibited: Paris, 1982, cat. no. 139; Lyons, 1983, cat. no. 70.

The photograph bottom left shows the model wearing the unfolded shawl wrapped round her, like a cape or cloak.

149

Design for a *burnous*
shawl.
Gonelle Frères, 1862.
Gouache on paper, 53 ×
25.2 cm/20⅞ × 10 in.
Paris, Musée des Arts
Décoratifs, Cabinet des
Dessins, no. CD5304,13.
Exhibited: Paris, 1982, cat.
no. 143.

In order to appreciate this
design, it is best to view it
horizontally: at the bottom
of the black field two small
pines face each other,
giving the impression of a
lion's mask topped by a
crown.

Design for a long shawl. Gonelle Frères, inscribed "made by Robert & Gosselin," 1862. Gouache on paper, 53.5 × 28 cm/21⅛ × 11 in. Paris, Musée des Arts Décoratifs, Cabinet des Dessins, no. CD5304,14. Exhibited: Paris, 1982, cat. no. 142.

Two large side panels curve around the central field, and between them is a motif of pines placed back to back; together they suggest the shape of an urn. The festooned frieze encompassing the black central field, is in turn surrounded by polychrome *mihrabs*, their apices pointing towards the center.

A signed design by Berrus for a long shawl.
Great Exhibition, London, 1862.
Gouache on paper, 49 × 20 cm/19¼ × 7⅞ in.
Paris, Musée National des Techniques, C.N.A.M., no. 8.799.

The design is symmetrical in relation to the vertical axis; only the deep end sections are mirror images along the horizontal axis. In the ends, four elongated pines, graduated in size, are conjoined with similar pines above a bunch of small pines which suggests a stylized tree of life. This bunch is echoed between the pines and a border which curves round in each corner, surrounded in turn by the outermost vertical and horizontal borders.

Long shawl design signed by Berrus. Paris Universal Exhibition, 1867. Gouache on paper, 54.8 × 26.9 cm/21½ × 10½ in. Paris, Musée des Arts Décoratifs, Cabinet des Dessins, no. CD5305.

In this design symmetry is total in relation to both axes. The black field is lozenge shaped and its points end in an ornamental motif shaped like a lily. The pines have become so misshapen in this composition that they are almost unrecognizable as such, contained within a frame of sweeping festoons.

Long shawl signed by
Berrus. Paris Universal
Exhibition, 1867.
Gouache on paper, 54.5 ×
26.6 cm/21½ × 10½ in.
Paris, Musée des Arts
Décoratifs, Cabinet des
Dessins, no. CD5306.

From 1867 onwards the
outline of decorative motifs
was sometimes
emphasized by narrow
white tracery. This design
is also completely
symmetrical in relation to
both axes. A bold fusiform
ornament stands out
against a rectangular
background; in its center
there is a medallion
towards which 12 small
pines with curled tops
converge in groups of
three.

Signed Berrus design for a
long shawl. Paris Universal
Exhibition, 1867.
Gouache on paper, 54.7 ×
26.6 cm/21½ × 10½ in.
Paris, Musée des Arts
Décoratifs, Cabinet des
Dessins, no. CD5308.

The same motif is placed in
relief in both halves of the
shawl; on one half it stands
out against a turquoise
background and on the
other against a sky blue
one.

Signed design by Berrus for an *à pivot* shawl.
Paris Universal Exhibition, 1867.
Gouache on paper, 97 × 40 cm/38⅛ × 15¾ in.
Paris, Musée des Arts Décoratifs, Cabinet des Dessins, no. CD5314.

This *à pivot* design comprises two pairs of pines, placed head to tail, occupying the whole length of the figured field. These S-shapes, which take the place of pines, cross a black central field which is also S-shaped. A black edging traces the outline of the motif and is in turn surrounded by a festooned border.

Design for a long shawl, signed Berrus.
Paris Universal Exhibition, 1867.
Gouache on paper, 50 × 23.5 cm/19¾ × 9¼ in.
Paris, Musée National des Techniques, C.N.A.M., no. 8.799.

The composition of this shawl design has been developed symmetrically around both axes. Backing on to both sides of a very stylized tree of life, is a pine with a base consisting of three segments and a curled tip ending in a flower motif.
The small black field is contained within a cruciform motif.

157

Long shawl design signed by Berrus.
Paris Universal Exhibition, 1867.
Gouache on paper, 88 × 36 cm/34⅝ × 14¼ in.
Paris, Musée National des Techniques, C.N.A.M., no. 8.799.
Exhibited: Paris, 1982, cat. no. 129.

The triple pine placed in the center of one half of the shawl is repeated in the other half by a rotation of 180 degrees, using the technique adopted for *à pivot* designs. The first niche is placed under a multifoil arch with three different ground colours.

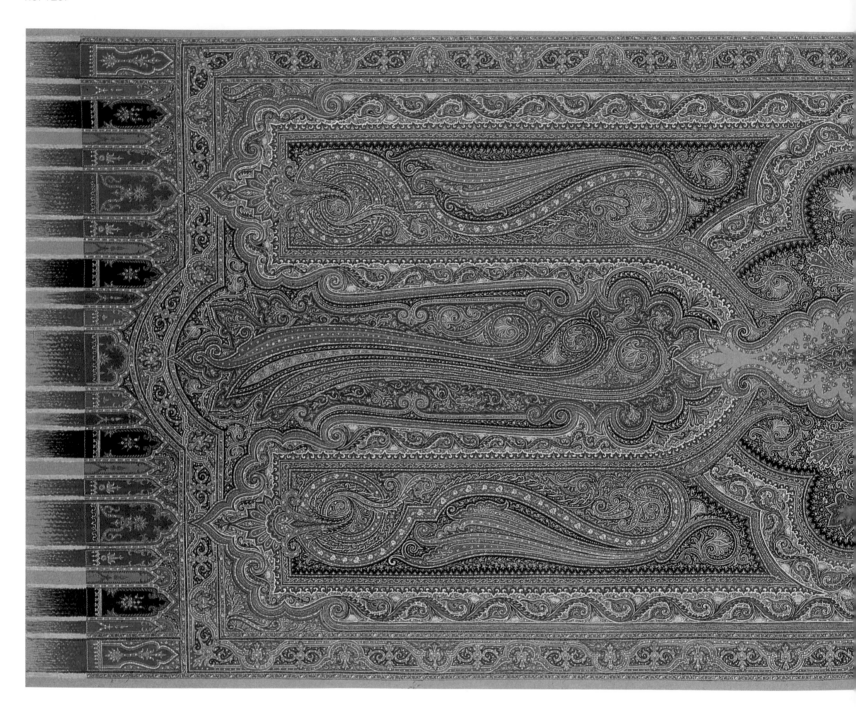

On page 160: long shawl (detail).
France, 1867, after a design by Berrus.
Woven *au lancé*, trimmed on back, cashmere (?), 356 × 164 cm/140⅛ × 64½ in.
Paris, A.E.D.T.A., no. 704.
Exhibited: Paris, 1982, cat. no. 117.

An unidentifiable mark has been woven in white into the small central field. The engraving (shown on page 161) is evidence that the shawl was designed by Berrus.

Below: quarter detail of long shawl design. Engraving of a shawl which was shown at the 1867 Paris Universal Exhibition, woven by the Paris manufacturers Bourgeois & Mahaut after a design by A. Berrus which was called the *Sun Shawl*. Published in the *Rapport des Délégations Ouvrières de l'Exposition Universelle de Paris, 1867*, in the chapter devoted to shawl designers.
Paris, library of the Musée des Arts Décoratifs.

Héliog.ᵉ Durand.   A. Berrus, inv.ᵗ   L. Le Maire sc

Right: quarter detail of a long shawl design, signed and dated by Berrus, 1866. Pencil, white gouache and gold highlights on paper, 72.5 × 44./ cm/28½ × 17½ in.
Paris, Musée des Arts Décoratifs, Cabinet des Dessins, no. CD5436,25.

Design for an *à pivot* long shawl (detail), signed by Berrus.
Paris Universal Exhibition, 1867.
Pencil and white gouache on paper, 95 × 44.5 cm/ 37⅜ × 17½ in.
Paris, Musée des Arts Décoratifs, Cabinet des Dessins, no. CD5436.30.

Sinuous pines twine around each other in this *à pivot* design, in the middle of which is a small white field. The borders surrounding this decoration look very like a carved wooden frame.

Design for a quarter of a long shawl by Berrus, not dated or signed. Pencil on paper, 73 × 47 cm/28¾ × 18½ in. Paris, Musée des Arts Décoratifs, Cabinet des Dessins, no. CD5436,26.

The most noticeable feature of this quarter detail is the giant festoon ornamentation, inside which are other, smaller festoons surrounding the decorative motif.

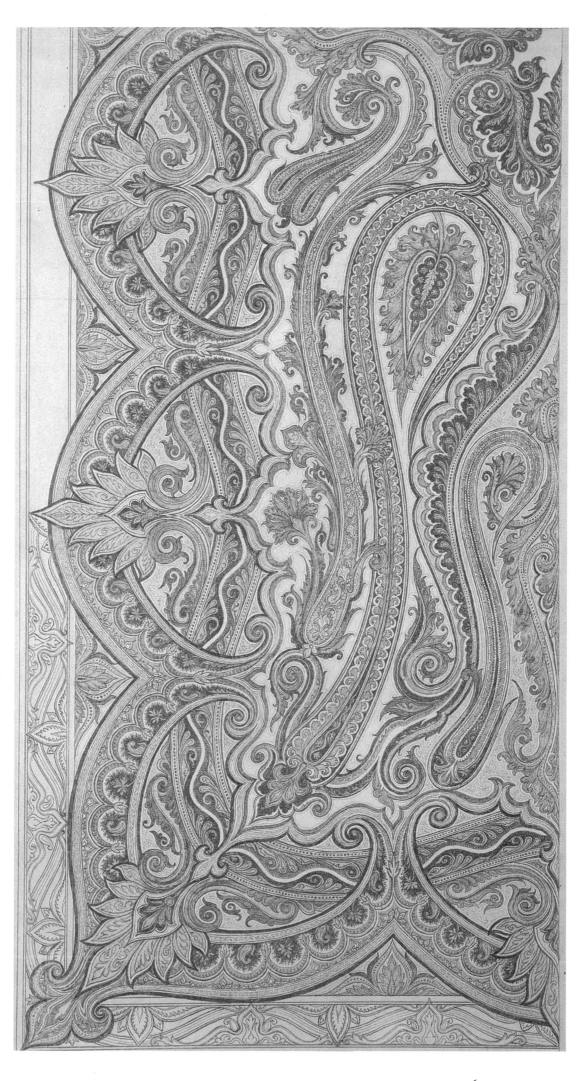

Design for a quarter of a long shawl by Berrus, not dated or signed.
Ink and gouache on blue paper, 73.7 × 50 cm/29 × 19¾ in.
Paris, Musée des Arts Décoratifs, Cabinet des Dessins, no. CD5436,39.

A bold spearhead motif points downwards and is entwined with plants tracing arabesques, reminiscent of traditional Celtic illumination in old Irish manuscripts. In the center of the motif are three slender interlaced pines.

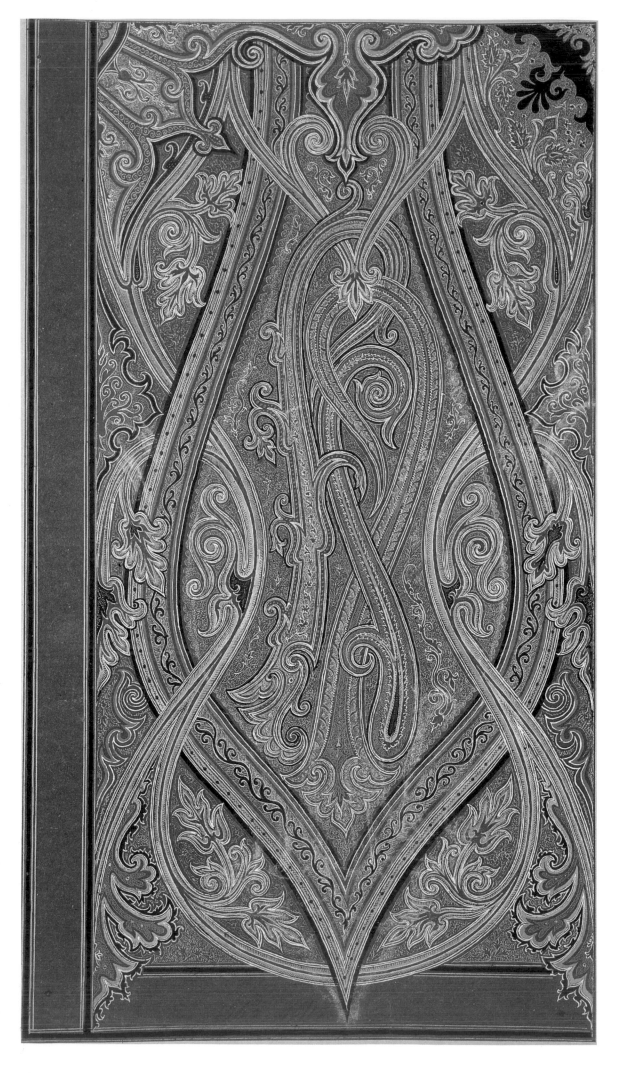

Long shawl design. Berrus, no date or signature. Ink and white gouache on blue paper, 64.5 × 35.4 cm/25⅜ × 14 in. Paris, Musée des Arts Décoratifs, Cabinet des Dessins, no. CD5436,42.

Pleated ornamental drapery directs the eye towards a large pedestal which encloses, among other decorative motifs, two confronted pines with split apices.

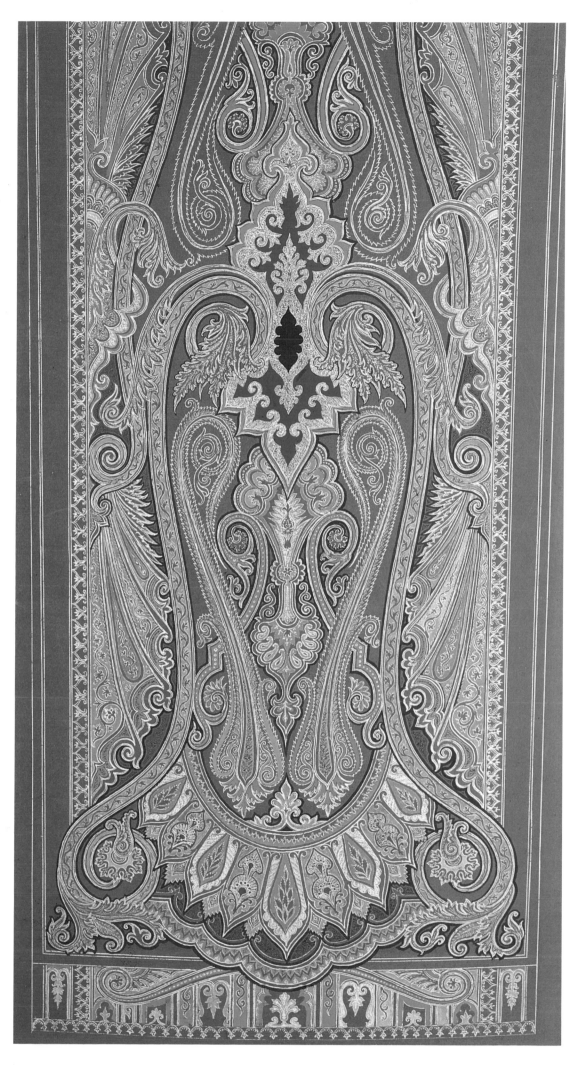

Design for a quarter of a long shawl by Berrus, no date or signature.
Ink and gouache on blue paper, 74 × 50 cm/29⅛ × 19¾ in.
Paris, Musée des Arts Décoratifs, Cabinet des Dessins, no. CD5436,40.

The effectiveness of this design owes much to the bold festoon which surrounds a shield motif. In the center of the latter a stylized tree of life can be discerned on the field in front of two pairs of intertwined pines.
The grid plan is visible; this made it possible to reproduce the design on a large sheet of paper, ready for the "*mise en carte*" process when the design was transferred to point-paper.

Long shawl design by Berrus, not signed or dated. Pencil and white gouache on paper, 58.2 × 35.8 cm/22⅞ × 14⅛ in. Paris, Musée des Arts Décoratifs, Cabinet des Dessins, no. CD5436,21.

This composition is contained within an elongated oval shape; in the center is a white, eight-pointed star-shaped field, forming the focal point for groups of pines which snake towards it.

Design for a long shawl by Berrus, not signed or dated.
Pencil on paper, 58 × 46.8 cm/22¾ × 18⅜ in.
Paris, Musée des Arts Décoratifs, Cabinet des Dessins, no. CD5436,23.

The central decoration is supported by two *rocaille* style columns enclosing a three-dimensional pine with a conical end. Some features are reminiscent of designs prepared for the 1855 Exhibition.

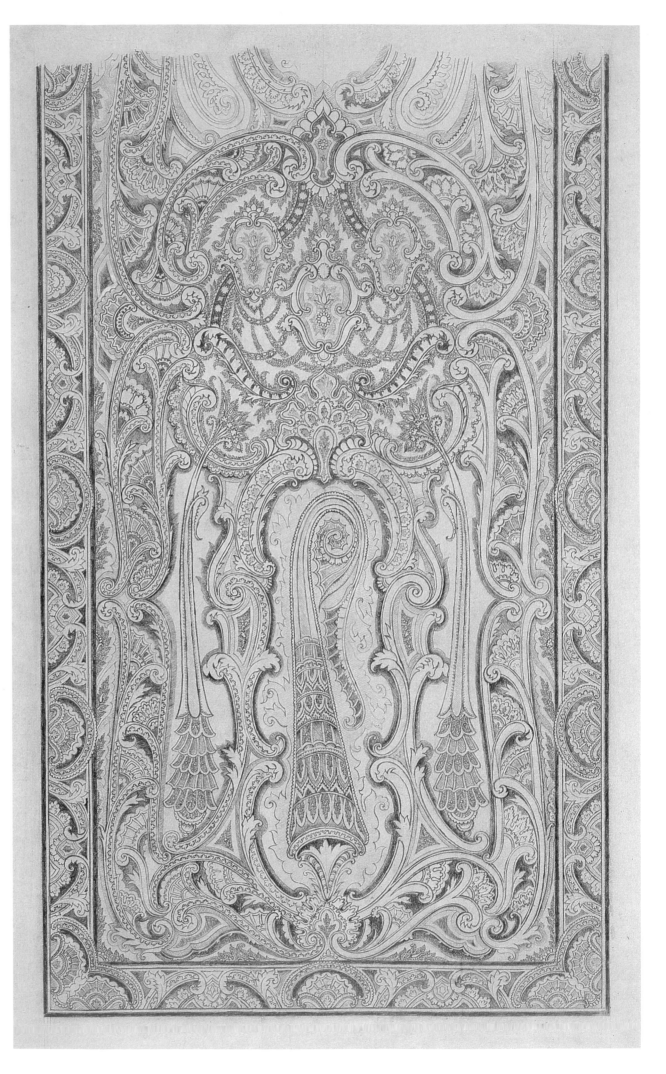

Design for a quarter of a long shawl by Victor Delaye. Engraving published in the *Album Indo-Parisien. Motifs des dessins industriels entièrement inédits*, Paris, n.d. (before 1867). Paris, Aux Fils du Temps.

This engraving is a good example of Victor Delaye's highly detailed work.

Signed shawl design by
Berrus. Vienna Universal
Exhibition, 1873.
Gouache on paper, 59.7 ×
31.5 cm/23½ × 12⅜ in.
Paris, Musée des Arts
Décoratifs, Cabinet des
Dessins, no. CD5312.

The design is
symmetrically arranged
around both axes. The
surround has a white
festoon edging; the deep
end (*pentes*) section is
decorated with two pines
arranged back to back on
either side of a spear-
shaped motif containing a
flowery ornament.

Signed shawl design by Berrus. Vienna Universal Exhibition, 1873. Gouache on paper, 51 × 22.5 cm/20 × 8⅞ in. Paris, Musée National des Techniques, C.N.A.M., no. 8.798.
Exhibited: Paris, 1982, cat. no. 129.

Another design which is symmetrically conceived in relation to both axes. The shawl's hooked pines face each other above a floral motif.

Design for an *à pivot* shawl, signed Berrus. Vienna Universal Exhibition, 1873. Gouache on paper, 106 × 42.3 cm/41¾ × 16⅝ in. Paris, Musée des Arts Décoratifs, Cabinet des Dessins, no. CD5313.

An oblong frame ending in two points contains two giant pines, positioned head to tail and aslant. A white outline, with flowers branching off it, crosses the pines and opens out in the center to form the reserve. Here Berrus was reworking a theme which he had used in his design for the 1867 Exhibition (shown on page 150, above).

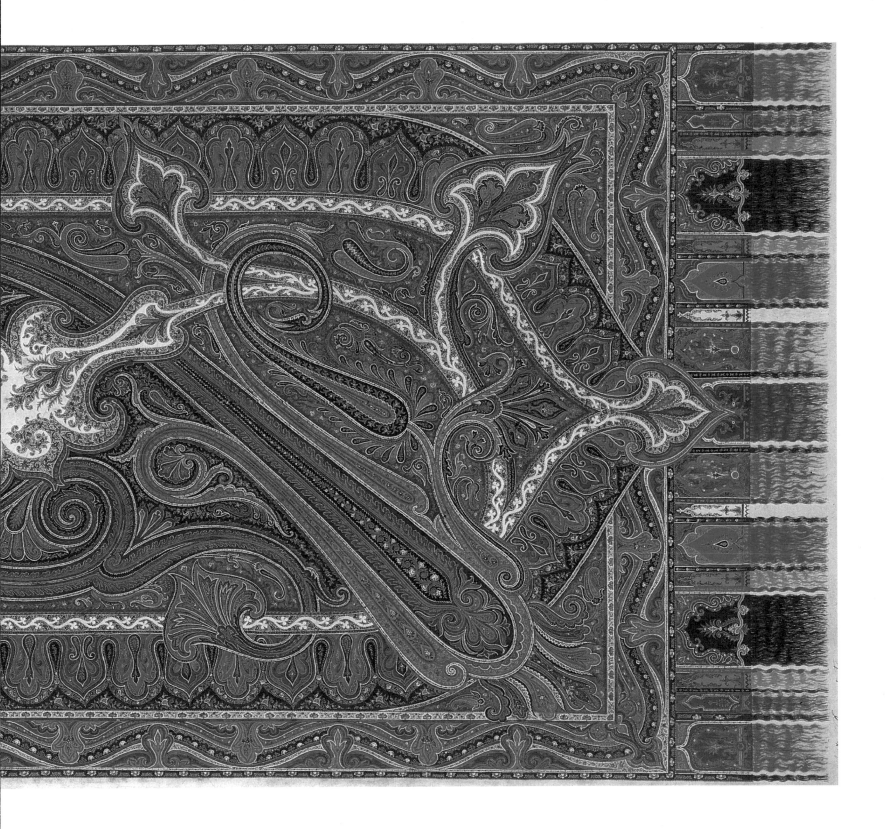

Signed shawl design by Berrus. Vienna Universal Exhibition, 1873.
Gouache on paper, 51 × 22.5 cm/20 × 8⅞ in.
Paris, Musée National des Techniques, C.N.A.M., no. 8.798.
Exhibited: Paris, 1982, cat. no. 129.

An arabesque of white outlines with floral motifs encircles pines which face each other across a motif topped by a lily.

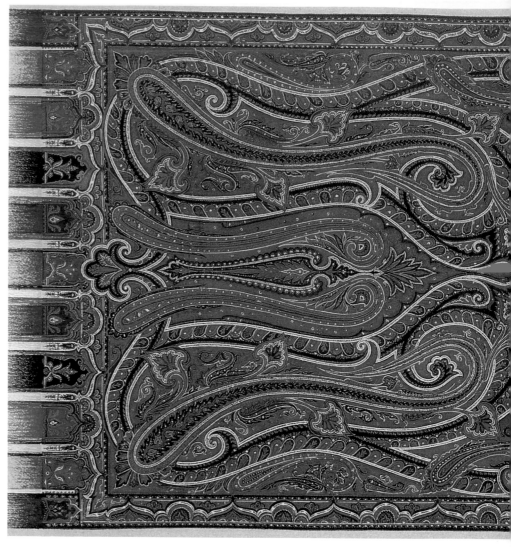

Shawl design signed by Berrus. Vienna Universal Exhibition, 1873.
Gouache on paper, 87 × 34 cm/34¼ × 13⅜ in.
Paris, Musée National des Techniques, C.N.A.M., no. 8.798.
Exhibited: Paris, 1982, cat. no. 129.

The lobes which radiate outwards from the central motif are in contrasting colours.

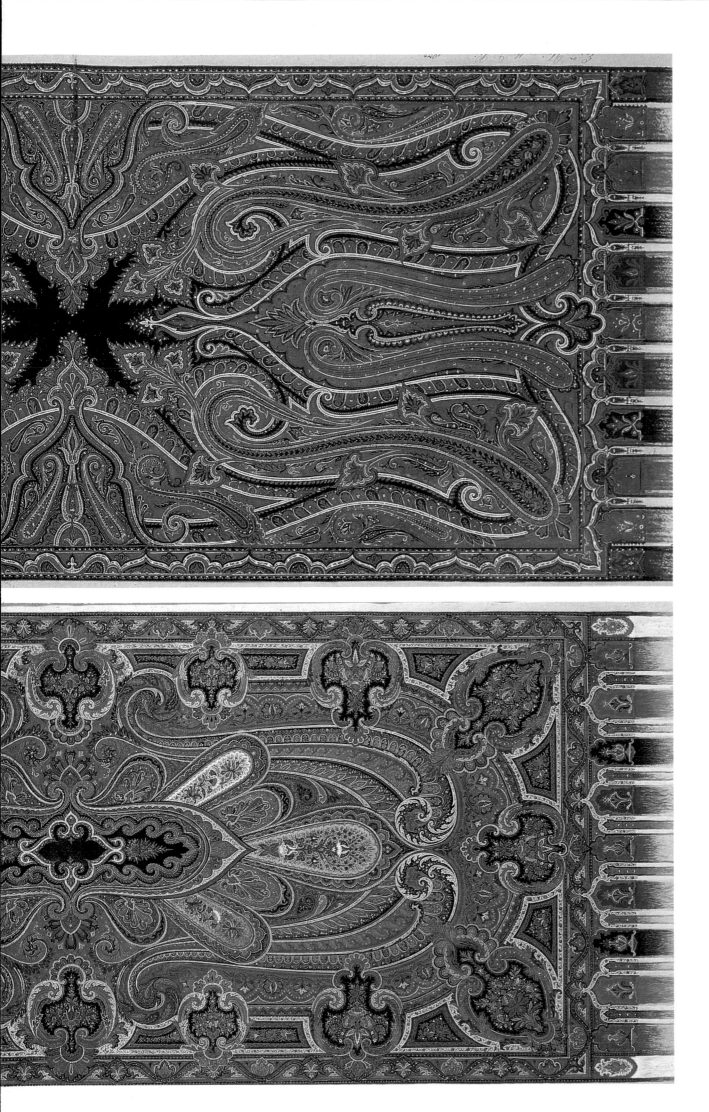

175

quare shawl.
orthwest India, c. 1870–
0.
will-tapestry woven in
everal pieces, cashmere,
10 × 204 cm/82⅝ ×
0¼ in.
Milan, Etro collection, no.
0.

This shawl was made up
from a number of small
motif "cut-outs," sewn
together like a patchwork
(see page 50) and
positioned regardless of
the grain of the weave,
making the shawl difficult
to smooth out and lay
completely flat. Note the
harlequin edges on all four
sides.

Opposite: center detail of
the shawl shown below.

Although a mark is clearly
visible and probably
indicates the workshop
where the shawl was
made, it has so far proved
indecipherable.

Long shawl (detail).
Europe, c. 1870–75.
Woven *au lancé*, trimmed
on back, wool, 340 × 164
cm/133⅞ × 64½ in.
Milan, Etro collection, no.
28.

This shawl has no reserve
or central field as such, its
place has been filled by a
central motif with a clear
outline. With the exception

of the harlequin shawl
ends, the warp is red. The
vertical borders have
circular motifs which call to
mind those representing
the Chinese *yin* and *yang*
symbols. A large stylized
flower is flanked on each
side by slim linked pines,
their apices curving to left
and right. Between their
bases grows another
flower, a stylized iris; these

pines have an Art Nouveau
feel to them.

Opposite: detail of the
large stylized flower
growing between the
linked pines in the shawl
shown above.

On pages 180–81: square
shawl with fully decorated
ground. France or Great
Britain, second half of the
nineteenth century.
Woven *au lancé*,

untrimmed back, silk, 180
× 180 cm/70⅞ × 70⅞ in.
Milan, Etro collection, no.
11.

In spite of its atypical
pattern, this style of shawl
also went under the name
of "cashmere."

Opposite: loom and tools
used by Kashmiri shawl
weavers.
Kashmir, mid nineteenth
century.
Watercolour drawing.
London, India Office
Library, Add. OR. 1729.

Marks, techniques, glossary, bibliography, index

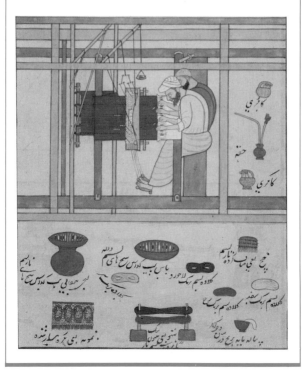

Woven and embroidered marks

Right: "H. Cachemire Pur," mark woven into the center of shawls manufactured by Frédéric Hébert from 1852.
Paris, author's collection, no. 39.

Far right: manufacturer's mark embroidered on a shawl woven in Kashmir; efforts to decipher these marks have so far proved fruitless.
Paris, author's collection, no. 71.

Right: "Cachemire," mark woven in a corner of a square shawl made by the Parisian manufacturer Laurent Biétry, from 1849.
Paris, Musée de l'Homme, Département d'Asie, no. 73.4.2.

Far right: "Biétry," mark woven in another corner of the same square shawl by the Paris manufacturer Biétry.

Right: "F.M.," the Parisian manufacturers Fortier & Maillard wove their initials into the corners of their shawls from about 1850 onwards.
Milan, Etro collection.

Far right: "G.F. Cie," the initials of the manufacturers Gaussen & Fargetton, Paris, were woven into the corners of their shawls from about 1850.
Paris, author's collection, no. 19.

Right: the Arms of England with the motto "*Honi soit qui mal y pense*" and "*Dieu et mon droit*" woven into the four corners of a long shawl (this detail is of a left-hand corner), made in 1855 to a design by Berrus.
Paris, author's collection, no. 42.

Far right: "Paris Exposition 1855" is the inscription woven into the two left-hand corners of this French rectangular shawl.
Milan, Etro collection, no. 58.

On shawl weaving in India

In his *Voyage dans l' Inde* (Travels in India), covering the years 1828–32, Victor Jacquemont describes his first encounter with shawl weavers in Ludhiana. His clear, precise description contains only one mistake: he uses the term weft when he means warp. This was a common error in those days and a contemporary historian of the shawl industry, Jean Rey, had already complained about it in 1823. The word weft has therefore been changed to warp wherever necessary in the following excerpts from Jacquemont's journal.

Ludhiana, February 14th, 1831
. . . The weaving manufactory is called a *dokan* or workshop. The warp is first stretched from a roller which rotates on the block of the loom. Ordinary shawls vary in width from 120–125 cm [47–49½ in]; three weavers work at the loom together, seated on a bench as long as the beam round which the warp is wound. Each weaver is in charge of at least seventy bobbins which he manipulates with the utmost dexterity if he is an experienced worker. Usually the man seated in the center is the most highly skilled; while carrying out his own work, he keeps an eye on that of his companions, points out their mistakes, guides and counsels them. This head weaver checks his own work by glancing at a pen and ink pattern tracing which shows the shape of the pines he is weaving but not their colours; while he is weaving he can see only the reverse side of his work. Unless he is exceptionally skilled, he keeps an old manuscript in front of him, well thumbed and greasy: from this he knows which bobbins to use, how many warp threads have to be lifted each time, etc.

The pines of Kashmir shawls, like the words of a language, are made up of a limited number of letters or syllables: they are simple shapes in themselves and it is the way in which they are arranged that produces the infinite variety of designs. The custom is for the children who work under the tutelage of a more experienced weaver to recite the words of this language as they read them; they say what they are doing as they complete each stage and they talk at some speed, to keep pace with the speed of their hands. The master weaver knows the lesson they are reciting by heart and he stops them at the slightest mistake and corrects them. A workshop has two, three or four looms, usually arranged in pairs facing one another. Shawls are always woven and sold in pairs, as like to one another as possible."

Kashmir, July 28th, 1831, Profits and taxes
The tax levied on shawls totals approximately 12 laks. One man collects the profit. He is always to be found in charge of a tribunal, assisted by experts and in the presence of all the shawl dealers.

All the shawls from the looms are brought here to be valued and before they are stamped and returned to their owners, the latter must pay one-quarter of their estimated value. If any clandestine weaving is discovered, very severe punishments are inflicted; as a result only narrow borders are woven in this way.

The "collector" has to send a twelfth of this revenue to Lahore each month and collect what is due to him on all finished goods; this is why he never waits till a shawl is finished before removing it from the loom. Each day his agents visit all the workshops and no sooner do they find that a few inches of shawl have been woven than they cut it off the loom and take it to their master for him to assess its value, stamp it and levy the tax. The weavers never manage to complete more than a meter of a shawl before the rapacious collector exacts his dues. This is why, of the thousands of shawls I have seen in Kashmir, every one without exception was made up of at least five pieces sewn together. The very costly shawls have their borders decorated with large pines

and the work is very fine, each shawl being made up of ten, twelve or even twenty pieces. Even the most inexperienced eye can, however, make out the joins since the pattern fragments are not sufficiently well matched. Although this would, to my mind, greatly lessen their value on the French market, it has no such effect in India or Persia. There are no exceptions to this practice here: for many years past all Kashmir shawls have been made by sewing pieces and fragments together.

The reprehensible, grasping behaviour of the *kardar* (the collector of shawl taxes) does not stem only from his obligation to remit a regular sum to Lahore covering the previous month's production but also from his constant fear that he may be supplanted without any warning at all and have to leave his successor with a windfall of untaxed production. The weavers have often volunteered to make progress payments for their work as it is completed, but since the tax is proportional to the estimated finished value of the shawl and this can only be assessed by the *kardar*'s public tribunal, with the help of his experts and the shawl dealers, there seems no option but to cut even small sections of woven material off the looms."

"Even without the absurd and hateful method of levying this tax, the *karkhandar* (the proprietor of the weaving factory) would still weave all his shawls in several pieces, except for the inferior quality shawls which could be woven from start to finish on the same loom within the space of four or five months. The finest *jamewars* [see glossary] and *dushalaks* [a pair of shawls] would have to stay on the same loom for years at a stretch (six, seven, even eight) before they were completed, so the borders of these are woven separately on other looms, as they are the pines and the background or *zamine*; this means they can be completed in one year."

The right side and the back of shawls

It is difficult to determine which weaving technique has been used when looking at the right side of a shawl; it is the back which contains the clues to how and where it was woven.

Right: right side of a twill-tapestry weave shawl. Kashmir, early nineteenth century.

Far right: back of the same twill-tapestry woven shawl; note the small two-colour ridges showing where the wefts, which do not pass from selvedge to selvedge, have been joined.

Below: right side of a shawl, woven *au lancé*, with pattern weft from selvedge to selvedge (with a trimmed back).
Europe, first third of the nineteenth century.

Far right: the trimmed back of the same shawl. The trimmed wefts have a roughish, velvety appearance.

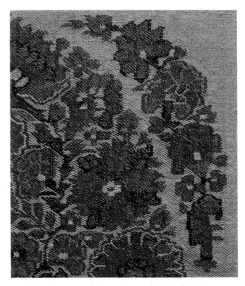

Twill

Twill weave is characterized by diagonal effects obtained by starting one warp thread further along for each sequence of a weft thread passing regularly over and under the warp threads.

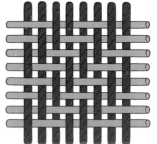
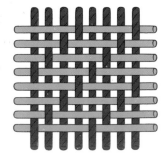

2/2 Twill
The weft threads (horizontal) pass successively over two warp threads (vertical) and under two warp threads.

3/1 Twill
The weft threads (horizontal) pass successively over three warp threads, and under one warp thread.

Espoliné weave in 2/2 twill, as carried out in Kashmir. In the decorated parts of the shawl, the colour wefts are interlinked, forming a two-coloured ridge on the back.

Glossary

Bobbin
Small wooden cylinder on which weft thread is wound for passing weft through the openings in the warp.

Border
The early shawls have several distinct borders:
Horizontal or cross border: narrow border parallel to the weft. An outer horizontal border comes between the main border and the fringes. An inner horizontal border sometimes comes between the main border and the field of the shawl.
Main border: deep border at the two ends of a long shawl, usually containing the pine motif which became known as the Paisley pattern.
Vertical or side border: narrow border parallel to the warp, running along each side of the shawl.

Cashmere
Term used for:
1) a shawl made in Kashmir
2) cashmere fiber, the wool of the shawl-goat
3) design derived from Indian shawls, hence, by association, European shawls so designed.

Corner motif
Pine or other ornament repeated in the four corners of the field.

Découpé
Trimmed or shorn. The term denotes that loose weft threads at the back of the shawl have been trimmed off.

Drawloom
Loom in which the pattern of the textile is determined by tying together those warp threads which come at the same point in each repeat of the pattern, so that they can be raised together by the drawboy who assists the weaver.

Ends
Narrow band of weaving at either end of a shawl between fringe and border
Harlequin ends: in these the band is woven in blocks of several different colours which extend into the fringe.

Espoliné
See twill-tapestry.

Field
Large area between the borders, the middle of the shawl, devoid of ornamentation or covered with small repeating patterns or stripes.

Fringe
Either formed of the warp protruding at each end of the shawl, or made separately and sewn on to the shawl.

Fringe-gates
Decorated ends developed from harlequin ends.

Gallery
Band of decoration based on the inner horizontal and vertical borders, running round the central field.
Inner gallery: further band of decoration within the gallery, encroaching on the field.

Jacquard
Attachment to the loom which dispenses with the drawboy, the warp threads raised to make the pattern being determined by a series of punched cards selecting hooks to operate the warp threads.

Jamewar
Indian term for a gown-piece, a shawl cloth with small repeating patterns, often striped, without any borders.

Au lancé
See weaving *au lancé.*

Paisley
See *pentes.*

Pashmina
Term applied to true Kashmirian shawl cloth of goat's wool.

Pentes
Term used to denote the two large areas of decoration between fringes and central reserve on later shawls which no longer have clearly defined end borders. There is no English equivalent.

Pine
The most common motif on Indian shawls, later known as the Paisley pattern.

Point-paper
Squared paper on which a design is worked out for weaving.

Printed warp
Warp printed before weaving to provide areas of different colour on a single thread.

Reserve
Small unpatterned area in the center of later shawls.

Selvedges
Very narrow, sometimes strengthened, strips of unpatterned weave at the sides of a shawl or piece of cloth.

Shawl
Derived from the Persian word *shal,* meaning cloth woven from fine wool. Types of shawl and shawl design are:
Burnous: shawl to be worn without folding, like a cape, the plain reserve being placed towards one side.
Filled ground: shawl completely covered with ornamentation, having no central reserve.
Harlequin shawl: in which the pines of the borders are in compartments each with a differently coloured ground.
Lopsided shawl: shawl with only one main border.
Medallion shawl: usually a square shawl with a medallion in the center and a quarter medallion repeated in each corner.
Pivoted pattern: on a long shawl, a design that repeats only once, turning 180 degrees in the center of the shawl to pivot about a central point.
Striped: shawl covered with stripes decorated with small motifs, with or without borders (see *jamewar*).
Turnover: square shawl, with wide borders sewn on two sides to form a right angle, and narrow borders similarly placed on the other two sides but sewn on back to front, both sets of borders showing their right sides when the shawl is folded in a triangle.

Shed
Opening in the warp, made by raising certain warp threads, through which the shuttle or bobbin is passed.

Tie-dyeing
Method of tying tightly bundles of warp threads to prevent dye from penetrating, so, after successive tying and dye baths, producing polychrome warp threads.

Twill
A weave in which the weft may pass not over one warp thread and under one, as in plain weave, but over two and under two, producing a herringbone effect, or over two or three warp threads and under one, the binding points of warp over weft in successive passes making diagonal lines across the cloth.

Twill-tapestry
A twill weave in which the weft does not pass from selvedge to selvedge but, as in tapestry, is turned back to form areas of colour interlinked at the edges.

Warp
Threads placed parallel between two beams on the loom, running lengthways in the finished cloth or shawl.

Weaving au lancé
Manner of weaving in which pattern wefts are passed from selvedge to selvedge.

Weaving espoliné
Weaving in twill-tapestry.

Weft
Threads passed at right angles to the warp, woven over and under the latter to form the cloth.

An anatomy of the shawl

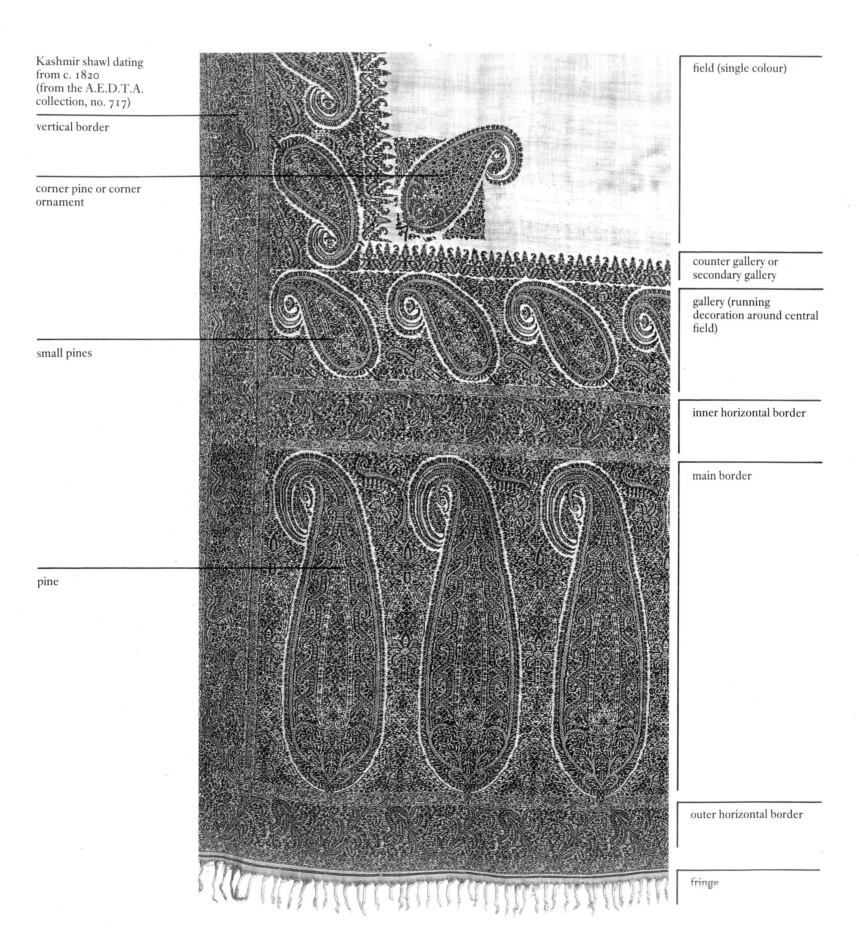

Kashmir shawl dating
from c. 1820
(from the A.E.D.T.A.
collection, no. 717)

vertical border

corner pine or corner
ornament

small pines

pine

field (single colour)

counter gallery or
secondary gallery

gallery (running
decoration around central
field)

inner horizontal border

main border

outer horizontal border

fringe

Dating nineteenth-century European shawls

Here are some suggested guidelines which may be of help when trying to date shawls. Obviously each feature, when considered in isolation, has only a relative value as a clue, in that it fixes a date before which the shawl could not have been woven. Only when several features of the shawl corroborate this evidence can a more definite date be postulated. When various elements of a shawl do not agree in what they tell us about the shawl's period of manufacture, then the most prudent course is to accept the latest possible date and explain those features which would suggest earlier dates by the producer's conservatism in retaining techniques or characteristics which belonged to an earlier era. It may well be, however, that the shawl is a composite creation, assembled from various pieces woven at different times.

These criteria are valid for the best quality, luxury market shawls which adopted different ornamentation as fashions changed. Examples manufactured for a less discerning market to less demanding standards are much more problematical and can only be dated by someone who is familiar with the development of products from each regional shawl-making industry.

Width of long shawls: from 1.30 m to 1.65 m/51¼ in to 65 in, widening steadily between 1800 and 1850.

Width of square shawls: increasing steadily from 1.35 m to 1.95 m/53⅛ in to 76¾ in, between 1800 and 1850.

Arrangement of pines: beginning with ten pines on the main border, the number was gradually reduced to eight, then seven (1830), and then six (1840); in three pairs, back to back or facing one another, then four (1850) grouped in two pairs, finishing with two giant pines (after 1865).

Height of the pines: these gradually increased in size from only 0.25 m to 1.20 m/9⅞ in to 47¼ in.

Width of the vertical border and horizontal border: from less than 2 cm/¾ in, at the beginning of the nineteenth century, these attained a maximum width of 18 cm/7⅛ in around 1840, and then gradually shrank to an average width of 10 cm/4 in.

Corner ornament: first appeared after 1810.

Gallery: introduced between 1815 and 1820; at first this running ornament only decorated the shorter sides of the single colour field; it was subsequently used on all four sides.

Secondary gallery: introduced after 1825. All this additional ornamentation inevitably reduced the size of the single colour field.

Harlequin fringes: first introduced on striped shawls, then adopted as fringe gates also in shawls with harlequin pines (1819). After 1834 all the best quality shawls were made with two harlequin shawl ends, comprising rectangles in several colours which were joined on regardless of the design of the shawl. After 1848 ornamentation was added to these rectangles which became square and then changed back to rectangles but arranged vertically (see 1867 shawl end, right, bottom).

Pure or true colour backgrounds: obtained by a special dye-press process for the warp threads before weaving, introduced in 1844.

Quartered shawls: after 1834.

Shawls "à pivot": after 1848.

Development of harlequin shawl ends

From 1820 harlequin shawls had multi-coloured fringe gates and fringes. As the century progressed, harlequin shawl ends grew steadily wider.

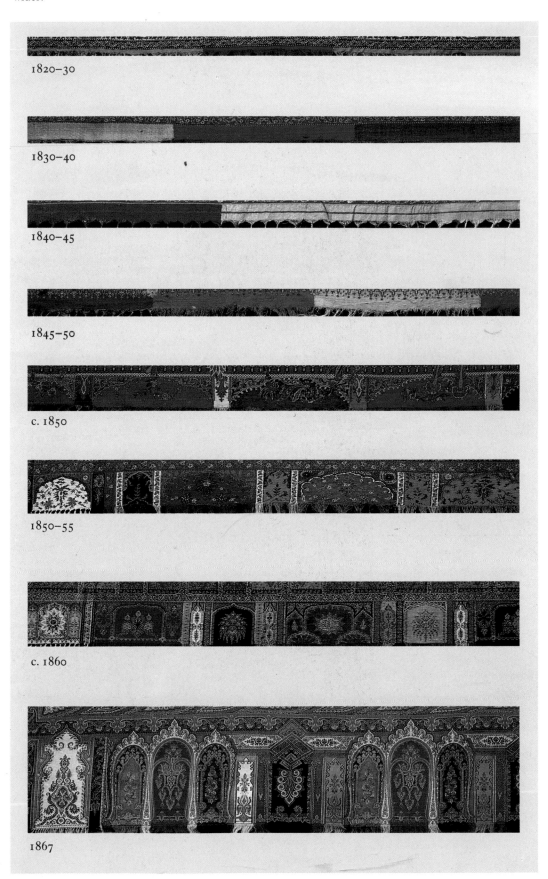

1820–30

1830–40

1840–45

1845–50

c. 1850

1850–55

c. 1860

1867

Bibliography

Abrantès, duchess of *Mémoires*, vol VI, Paris, 1835

Ames, F. *The Kashmir Shawl and its Indo-French Influence*, Woodbridge, Suffolk, 1986

Anavian, R. and G. *Royal Persian and Kashmir Brocades*, Kyoto, 1975

Anon. *Mémoires et souvenirs d'une femme de qualité sous le consulat et l'Empire*, Paris, 1966

The Art of Shawl, exhibition catalogue, West Surrey College of Art and Design, 1977

Balzac, H. de *La Comédie Humaine*, 1st ed., Paris, 1844

Bernier, F. *Voyage dans les Etats du Grand Mogol*, Paris, 1981 (1st ed. 1670–71)

Bezon, M. *Dictionnaire Général des Tissus anciens et modernes*, Paris, 1856–63

Biétry, L. *Réponse à une brochure d'un fabricant de châles, le châle cachemire français, le châle des Indes et la marque de fabrique*, Paris, 1849

Blair, M. *The Paisley Shawl and the Men who Produced it*, Paisley, 1904

Boigne, C.-L.-E.-A. *Mémoires de la comtesse de Boigne, née d'Osmond*, Paris, 1979 (1st ed. 1907)

Bordini, S. "Amédée Couder et l'architecture et l'industrie comme moyen de perfection sociale", in *Storia dell'Arte*, n. 30–31, 1977

Le Châle cachemire en France au XIXᵉ siècle, exhibition catalogue, Musée Historique des Tissus, Lyons, 1983–84

Champeaux, A. de "Les Artistes de l'Industrie", in *Revue des Arts Décoratifs*, vol. X, Paris, 1889–90

Clabburn, P. *Shawls in Imitation of the Indian*, Shire Album 77, 1981

Couder, A. *Analyse du dessin des cachemires et moyens de rendre les schalls français supérieurs à ceux des Indes*, Paris, 1834

Couder, A. *Notices explicatives de ses dessins exposés au Conservatoire Impérial des Arts et Métiers*, undated MS kept at The Conservatoire National des Arts et Métiers, Paris

Cross, W. "Descriptive Sketch of Changes in the Style of Paisley Shawls . . .", in *The Paisley and Renfrewshire Gazette*, 1872

Delaye, V. *Album Indo-Parisien. Motifs de Dessins industriels entièrement inédits*, Paris, n.d. (before 1867)

Deneirouse *Traité sur la fabrication des châles des Indes*, Paris, 1851

Deneirouse *Notice sur la nécessité de remplacer par un tissage mécanique les brochés à la main*, Paris, 1863

Falcot, P. *Traité encyclopédique et méthodique de la Fabrication des Tissus*, 2nd ed., Mulhouse, 1852

Fleury Chavant *Album du Cachemirien*, Paris, 1837

Fleury Chavant *Souvenir de l'Exposition des Produits de l'Industrie française, 1839*, Paris, 1839

Goncourt, E. de *La Maison d'un artiste*, Paris, 1880

Gordejewa, O. *Russian kerchiefs and shawls*, Leningrad, 1986

Hirayama *Tissage Cachemire*, Tokyo, 1985

Hügel, C. F. von *Kaschmir und das Reich der Siek*, Stuttgart, 1840

Indian and European Shawls, exhibition catalogue, Antique Textile Company, London, 1982

Irwin, J. *Shawls, a Study in Indo-European Influences*, London, 1955

Irwin, J. *The Kashmir Shawl*, London, 1973 (1st ed. 1955)

Jacquemont, V. *Voyage dans l'Inde pendant les années 1828–1832*, Paris, 1841

The Kashmir Shawl, exhibition catalogue, Yale University Art Gallery, 1975

Kashmirsjaals, exhibition catalogue, Haags Gemeentemuseum, the Hague, 1985–86

Labiche, E. *Le Cachemire X.B.T.*, in *Théâtre complet*, vol. VI, Paris, 1892

Le Play, F. *Le Tisseur en châles de Paris*, in *Les Ouvriers Européens*, Paris, 1887

Lomüller, L. *Guillaume Ternaux 1763–1833, créateur de la première intégration industrielle française*, Paris, 1978

Maze-Censier, L. *Les Fournisseurs de Napoléon et des deux impératrices*, Paris, 1893

La Mode du châle cachemire en France, exhibition catalogue, Musée de la Mode et du Costume, Paris, 1982

Peyot, M. F. *Cours complet de Fabrique pour les Etoffes de soie*, Lyons, 1866

Polonceau *Notice sur les chèvres asiatiques à duvet de cachemire*, Versailles, 1824

Records of the commissioners of the Exhibitions, Paris, 1801, 1806, 1819, 1823, 1827, 1834, 1839, 1844, 1849

Records of the commissioners of the Great Exhibitions, London, 1851, 1862; Paris, 1855, 1867, 1878; Vienna, 1873

Rey, J. *Etudes pour servir à l'histoire des châles*, Paris, 1823

Rock, C. H. *Paisley Shawls. A Chapter of the Industrial Revolution*, Paisley, 1966

Rossbach, E. *The Art of Paisley*, New York, 1980

Stack, L. "Two Types of Reversible Shawls", in *Bulletin de liaison du Centre d'Etude des Textiles Anciens*, no. 45, Lyons, 1977

Tessier, M. "Mémoire sur l'Importation en France des chèvres à duvet de Cachemire", in *Annales de l'Agriculture Française*, second series, vol XI, Paris, 1819

Van Gennep, A. *Manuel de folklore français*, Paris, 1938–58

Vigée Le Brun, L. E. *Souvenirs de Madame Vigée Le Brun*, Paris, n.d.

Vigne, G. T. *Travels in Kashmir*, London, 1842

Völker, A. "Die Produktion von 'Wiener Shawls' in der ersten Hälfte des 19. Jahrhunderts", in *Documenta Textilia*, n. 7, Monaco, 1981

Wallis, G. *The Exhibition of Art-Industry in Paris, 1855*, London, 1855

Whyte, D. "Edinburgh Shawls and their Makers", in *Costume. The Journal of the Costume Society*, no. 10, 1976

Index

Picture Sources

All the photographs in this book are by Massimo Listri, except for the following:

Artothek (Joachim Blauel), Planegg, 18
Studio Basset, Lyons, 29, 45a, 45b
Bibliothèque Nationale, Paris, 34, 38a, 38b, 39
British Library, London, 183
Michel de Lorenzo, Vence, 24
Lauros-Giraudon, Paris, 36
Musées de la Ville de Paris © SPADEM 1986, 2
Philadelphia Museum of Art, 47
Pozzar, Trieste, 35
Service photographique de la Réunion des musées nationaux, Paris, 17, 23, 33, 49
Philippe Valldemosa, Paris, 90, 91
Victoria and Albert Museum, London, 81

The weaving examples on page 186 by Gabriel

Vial, C.I.E.T.A. (Centre International pour l'Etude des Textiles Anciens), Musée Historique des Tissus, Lyons, were drawn by Roberto Maresca.

Acknowledgements

The Publisher wishes to thank the following institutions and collectors for allowing Massimo Listri to photograph their property:

Musée du Louvre, Paris
Conservatoire National des Arts et Métiers (C.N.A.M.), Paris
Musée de la Mode et du Costume de la Ville de Paris, Paris
Musée de l'Homme, Paris
Musée des Arts Décoratifs, Paris
Bibliothèque Forney, Paris
A.E.D.T.A. (Association pour l'Etude et la Documentation des Textiles d'Asie), Paris
Aux Fils du Temps, Paris
Gerolamo Etro, Milan
Monique Lévi-Strauss, Paris